HIGHLAND SPRING

HIGHLAND SPRING

W. R. Mitchell

ROBERT HALE & COMPANY

First published in Great Britain 1972

ISBN 0 7091 3462 2

Robert Hale & Company
63 Old Brompton Road
London, S.W.7

For
JANET

PRINTED IN GREAT BRITAIN BY
CLARKE, DOBLE & BRENDON LTD.
PLYMOUTH

CONTENTS

ILLUSTRATIONS

MAPS

PICTURE CREDITS

Author: 1, 4, 5, 7, 13, 16, 19, 20, 21, 22, 27, 28, 30; British
Museum: 9; Alex C. Cowper (courtesy of the Highland Cattle
Society): 10; the Forestry Commission: 2; Arthur Gilpin: 15;
R. Goodier: 14; Bill Grant: 11, 17, 18, 29; Dick Hilton: 3; Eric
Hosking: 8, 26; J. A. McCook (courtesy of RSPB): 23; Lea
MacNally: 24, 25; Geoffrey N. Wright: 6, 12.

INTRODUCTION

Spring can be tardy, irresolute, in the Central Highlands of Scotland.

A true northern spring, it surges uneasily, to and fro, across the glens and straths. It then has to fight its way yard by yard to the Cairngorm barrens. Here, on the highest range of hills in Britain, spring may be nothing more than a good-natured wink between winter and summer.

A full month after spring has burgeoned in southern England, deciduous trees in the upper valley of the Spey stand with skeletal bareness. By day, a hard northern light illuminates the wizened vegetation. A visitor might find himself shivering at the approach of night, even a short June night.

I journeyed to the Highlands in late May, when theoretically they should at least have been 'aired'. Winter lingered in the ice I scraped from the windows of my car following an overnight stop at Pitlochry; it was detectable in the chattering teeth of the angler striding from the 'snow water' of the Spey near Grantown and in the snowflakes swirling in high corries on the Cairngorms, where snow buntings—also called 'snowflakes' in the picturesque language of the northlands—sometimes build nests under the jumbled grey stones.

At lower levels, the spring sunshine draws a responsive reddish glow from Scots pines in the few relict areas of the old Caledonian Forest.

Calendar dates mean little. I quickly discounted them. When, indeed, does the Highland spring really begin?

In March, the first shrill-voiced oyster-catchers are following the line of the Spey from the Moray coast, and some of these handsome pied birds with beaks long and red, like sticks of sealing wax, will nest on gravel beds over eighty miles from the sea. The *kleeping* of oyster-catchers helps to break the winter silence. The up-river journey is made more laboriously by salmon moving on the spawning run to the high hills.

Ravens on the sheep ranges of the Monadhliath are poking at the remnants of last year's nests, and planning additions, long before the official arrival of spring. The ravens let the thermals carry them high, and then the birds dive or even turn on their backs as they are swept by the fervour of courtship or by the sheer zest for life. The *pruk* of the raven echoes weirdly from above the banks of mist. At some time while incubating its eggs, the raven will flick snow from wings as black as an undertaker's suit.

In most years, the crossbills of the pine forests are freed from worries about food, collecting seeds at will. These curious birds with the twisted mandibles can nest in advance of the true spring. They are courting in March. Young crossbills have often reached the point of independence when some other species of birds are engaged in the nesting preliminaries.

Golden eagles anticipate the calendar spring. The eggs are laid in mid-March, prior to which the birds patched up their gargantuan nests that straddle cliff ledges or, fairly commonly in the region of the Spey, are set among the branches of remote Scots pines.

In March, the red deer are in 'starvation month' when there is little fresh grazing to be had. Later the stags drop their antlers and move up the hills in anticipation of rich spring and summer grazing in the corries and alpine meadows. Wheatears *chack* on the still-frosted heights. Dippers have built domed nests where the burns run white with fury at the start of the thaw.

The voices of wading birds animate the vast tracts of moorland where, during winter, little more was heard beyond the becking of red grouse and the gruff voices of the hooded crows. Greenshanks nest in a few wild, empty places. Golden plover whistle, rather sadly it always seems to me, on well-fleshed hills such as those above the Drumochter Pass. There are demonstrative lapwings and curlews in the meadows.

Late in March the cock capercaillie, largest grouse in the world, struts in the forest glades. Jerking back its head, drooping its wings, elevating and fanning its tail, the caper utters a medley of sounds that are like echoes from pre-history. From the tousled marginal land beyond the pines comes the *coo-rooing* of showy blackcocks.

Winter usually lingers into April. Flocks of snow buntings lose none of their cheerfulness in the grim conditions of the 'tops'. The birds twitter gaily when they are tossed by bitter winds sweeping the plateaux and hill edges. The buntings wintering in the Highlands come mainly from Greenland and Scandinavia. They will be among the first birds to break into the far northern stillness.

When a moderating climate is felt in the glens and gorges, there remain the 'islands' of Arctic-type landscape around and over 4,000 feet above sea level. Here, in April, the ptarmigan cease to be gregarious. Cock birds stake territorial claims, and belch abuse at rivals. Ptarmigan live in a world of pink granite and diminutive plants.

The ospreys return to Loch Garten. Wild cats drop their kittens in lairs set among the rocks at about 1,000 feet above sea level. Woodcock fly their evening circuits, each bird advertising itself at intervals by uttering three grunts and a squeak.

In late May, sandpipers display beside the lochans and willow warblers sing almost everywhere in forest and wood, as they have done since trees first rooted in Highland Scotland following the retreat of the ice sheets. Crested tits feed their young in holes bored in the rotten stumps of pines deep in Abernethy, Glen More and the other ancient Speyside forests. Hen capercaillie, also in a world of pine and heather, cover their eggs like feathered tea cosies.

There is a freshness about the Highland spring. High summer seems jaded by comparison with this season of awakening, and I usually ignore it. Early tourists tended to arrive in September and October, when the bracken has died back and become yellow and orange; when the birches hold out branches full of golden leaves that shimmer in the lightest breeze; when the air is fresh again after the summertime lethargy.

During part of my latest spring jaunt, I stayed at a guest house a mile or two from Aviemore. Awakening at 4.45 am, I looked through the window of my wee room just under the slates and saw that it framed a view of the Cairngorms. The whaleback forms lay about seven miles away. Here the conditions are invariably wild and fierce, yet their smooth lines and the early morning mist had softened them. I gazed at 300-million-year-old rock, the exposed and enduring roots of a mountain system that once was infinitely higher.

Part of Rothiemurchus, the 'great plain of the pines', lay before me. Here were airy pine woods and stretches where pines polka-dotted heather moorland. In the early sunlight, Rothiemurchus appeared to smoulder with tones of yellow and brown that offset the bottle-green crowns of the pines.

Now I looked downwards. Red squirrels performed acrobatics on the garden fence in front of the guest house. At the back, beyond a lochan, a roe deer tripped across a dewy meadow. The area rang with curlew calls—the sharp, silvered calls of alarm, sometimes rising to a yelp, rather than the drawling call which inspired a Gaelic name meaning 'the weeping one'. The lapwing nesting in the lowlands as well as on the gentler hill slopes is the subject of another tender Gaelic belief—that each bird holds the soul of a young woman who died in childbirth. The idea possibly sprang from the plaintive manner and call of a disturbed lapwing circling its nest.

I left the guest house and walked near some pines. Crossbills were feeding, springing the scales of green cones. The family party at breakfast included pink cock, green hen, sombre-brown youngsters. In any other surroundings but a Scots pine or larch they would have invited attention. Here they were unobtrusive.

The Highlands appeal to me because they are big, broad, elemental—refreshingly empty of people in spring. Then you have space in which to move even in Glen More, for spring proper is a time between the winter sport of ski-ing and the summer sport of mass tourism. Scotland as a whole is only about three-fifths the size of England. To me it appears to be infinitely larger.

A Sassenach who writes about Highland Scotland can easily discomfort a great company of Scottish writers who have served the area well. They tend to comment on an Englishman's lack of sensitivity about matters north of the Highland Line. Yet even an Englishman must be allowed the joy of recording his experience and discoveries in Old Caledonia.

Sassenach is a Highlander's disrespectful term for a Lowlander—not specifically an Englishman. It means, I understand, a 'fat, gluttonous fellow', and the implication is that Lowlanders are as soft as the countryside in which they live.

I am a hill man, by birth and temperament, born in the shadow of the Pennines and frequently recreating in the Lake District. A love of wild hills, their birds and beasts, has drawn me to Highland Scotland again and again.

1

A TASTE OF THE HIGHLANDS

Towards the end of the eighteenth century, when Highland tempers were still high following the wreck of the Jacobite cause, Colonel Thomas Thornton, who lived near Knaresborough, in Yorkshire, made *A Sporting Tour through the northern parts of England and great part of the Highlands of Scotland.* This was the cumbersome title of his book and recollections, published in 1804.

We do not know precisely in which year Colonel Thornton entered wildest Scotland—it could have been 1785 or 1786—but his book helped to popularize the region among shooters and anglers. And it contains some word pictures of the Highlands before the days of organized tourism.

A naturalist of today will care little for Colonel Thornton. He was that type of Regency character lacking every virtue except physical bravery. By our standards he was irresponsible and frivolous. His military title means little by itself, for in the eighteenth century a man could buy his way up the scale from Ensign to Lieutenant-Colonel. It is apparent that Colonel Thornton had means at the time in which we are interested, and his excesses and subsequent bankruptcy are another story.

The Colonel and his friends went to Scotland with the express purpose of blasting a sporting way from glen to glen and from crag to crag. They flew hawks and also fished, mainly for pike. What delighted me about the book—and stimulated me to undertake this Highland jaunt—was its impressions of life in the Highlands at a time when, to quote Colonel Thornton, "they have been hitherto but little explored". To the attentive traveller, they offered a rich field for observation. The sportsman would find in the region "an inexhaustible fund of amusement".

Nature in the Highlands assumed a bolder style. "Rocks are everywhere heaped on rocks and present, with the immense lakes, or rather seas, which they encircle, scenes the most interesting and sublime. . . . Fish and game of different kinds are everywhere found in abundance."

Spending much of his time in Badenoch, by the upper Spey, the Colonel noticed the climatic differences to be found with increasing altitude. "The tops of their lofty mountains are certainly buried, as it were, in eternal snows; but their altitude does not affect the valleys. Here, being protected by immense mountains, clothed with impenetrable forests, they are warmer than in most situations."

Colonel Thornton guided me through the Highlands as they were before a veneer of romanticism had been added. He travelled through the wilderness as comfortably as possible, using a gig and two baggage wagons. The party included some friends, a valet, wagoner, falconer, boy, "and other servants". He blazed his own tourist trail.

The remoteness of the Highlands in the eighteenth century can be deduced from the fact that the Colonel chartered the sloop *Falcon*, "manned with a master and two mariners", to carry his necessary apparatus from York to Hull and thence to the Moray coast. He had bought two boats "for the purpose of navigating the lakes and fishing". His other equipment, including tents, was such that "three or four gentlemen, with their servants, hawks, dogs, nets, guns, &c., could be accommodated whenever they saw any beautiful spot that promised to afford them sport, and might halt as long as they pleased, without being obliged to trust in the precarious entertainment of an inn".

The *Falcon* sprang a leak off the Yorkshire coast, but managed to reach Whitby harbour, where the repairs were made in two days. At Forres, the equipment was transferred into forty-nine

Rough path between Scots pine and blaeberry in the Black Wood of Rannoch

Scots pine—one of the elite trees in the Black Wood of Rannoch

small carriages for movement to Badenoch. The boats were borne on horse-drawn sleds.

The Colonel checked his stores: hams, bacon, reindeer and other tongues, soaked beef, pigs' countenances, pickles and sweetmeats, biscuits. There were tents and equipment, all kinds of nets, six hawks, fours setters, six pointers and a deer hound. In the armoury were two double-barrelled guns, a rifle and three "single barrels", 40 pounds of dry powder, 40 pounds of powder "rather damp", 11 bags of shot and flints.

The Colonel clearly recalled that moment in his journey when he felt that the Highlands were near. Near the Clyde he swallowed a little "half-Highland air" and walked "only four miles from the bridge of Freume, which divides the Highlands from what is called, here, the low country".

I got my first whiff of the Highlands a few miles from Crieff, which is the capital of Strathearn. The road to Dunkeld entered the Sma' Glen. This gorge in the lumpy Ochil Hills may be small by Highland standards but delights a traveller who has just crossed the rolling uplands of the Borders and sped across a plain or two. The Gaelic name is more expressive; it means a glen that is narrow, not small.

To the left soared curvacious hills, with dark grey crags and heather sprouting from crack and ledge. The slopes to my right looked more abrupt. Here were more crags, with fan-shaped screes. Tumbling water was flanked by stretches of emerald grass that shouted to be noticed in this dun-coloured area.

Beyond the glen lay more hills. I had been warned not to call a Scottish peak a mountain. It is a hill—or a ben (from the Gaelic *beinn*) if you wish. My journey had scarcely begun and I was being confronted by Scottish Gaelic, the regular speech of only a few thousand people which remains the language of topography. The maps of Scotland are strewn with the adjectives of a dying language. In Strathspey I would hear Northern Scots, which is a variety of the Lowland speech.

At the Sma' Glen I first pondered on the Highland Line, the edge of the Grampian scarps, product of a geological fault running diagonally from north-east to south-west. There is a

B

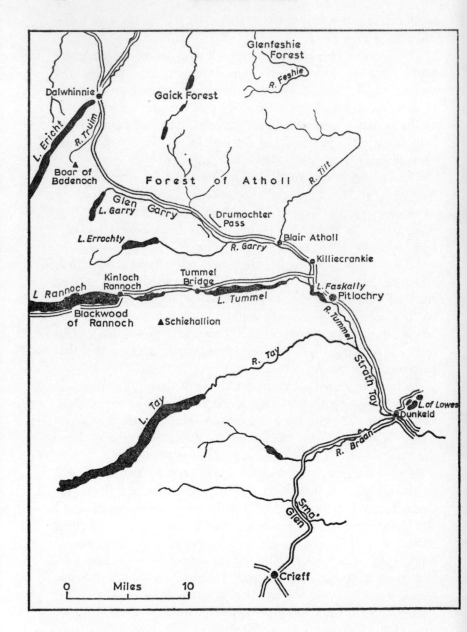

complementary diagonal in the line of the Scottish border with England, from Tweed to Solway. The Highland Line also represents the division between two cultures. Beyond it, centuries ago, was a lost world—craggy hills, pine forest, lochan, swamp. If Agricola and Severus did lead Roman troops into northern Scotland, as some historians claim, they must have been startled by the primitive savagery of old Caledonia.

I had promised myself that I would not become involved with Scottish history. Even devout Scotsmen argue incessantly about its finer points. Yet there was something about the Sma' Glen and its Ochil setting that stimulated thought about Scotland's past—about the people called Scotti who migrated here from Ireland; about a gentle Celtic saint, Columba, and his civilizing influence in the Highlands. Columba trudged from Iona to Inverness in 565 AD and preached before the King of the Picts. Traditionally, St Columba baptized the king and his men at the root of a young fir tree. Fir was the old term for Scots pine.

Highland Scotland, for long governed in accordance with clan divisions, and based on the Gaelic culture, has borne great sadness since the abortive Jacobite risings. Following them, the chief was no longer the supreme symbol of clan authority; central government called the tune.

Romanticism had entered my soul. The vista beyond the Sma' Glen, and the sight of Highland cattle, chestnut-brown against the freshening green of a pocket among the hills, evoked thoughts of Rob Roy, big-boned and with flaming red hair. The first Scotsman I met was a small, dark, sharp-featured Celtic type! Romanticism flowered with Sir Walter Scott and received royal patronage when the Prince Consort built a fairy-tale castle in the upper valley of the Dee.

In the fertile, rolling countryside beyond the Sma' Glen the road passed down short avenues of hardwoods, many of the trees being oak. The buildings I saw varied in size and stature, from gentlemen's houses, in neat and squared-up stone, to long and low farmsteads, grey-slated, white-walled, some with outbuildings formed of rough wooden sides, the roofs being of corrugated iron painted red, and that no longer the fiery red it had been when first applied.

The road began to dip towards the Tay at Dunkeld. Now I saw conifers in dense stands. The craggy hills were standing up to their necks in spruce and pine, part of an afforestation programme that Wordsworth would have described as "vegetable manufactory". I have read somewhere of the modern obsession with "pine, poles and pulp".

Yet conifers are appropriate to this wild northern landscape; they are hardy primitives, with naked seeds protected from the weather by scales. Scotland has more conifers than broad-leaved trees and, in the north-east, the greatest density of woodland in Britain. Strangely, the most popular species in tree-planting programmes is not a native of Britain, nor even of the Continent, which might be expected to do well on home ground. Foresters plant millions of the sitka spruce, which hails from British Columbia and Alaska. The Douglas fir is another New World species I saw in the Highlands, and this was unknown in Britain before 1827.

I descended to Dunkeld, saw a sparkle on the Tay (which, with a length of 118 miles, is the longest river in Scotland) and crossed Telford's elegant bridge, which was completed in 1809. Dunkeld was then described as "the portal of the Central Highlands". Once it was a centre of Pictland, "dun" being the Pictish name for fort. The people of ancient Caledonia, known to the Romans as Picti, were fair-complexioned, big-boned, with flaming red hair and tattooed bodies. Cata noted that they revelled in war and witty conversation. They are remembered but faintly. Time has almost obliterated their language.

At Dunkeld I looked for a special kind of larch. A gamekeeper who has spent 30 years "south of the Border" told me of his apprenticeship days in this valley of the Tay and described larches brought here in 1738 by the Menzies of Culdares. They were reputedly the first larch trees to be planted in Britain. At Dunkeld, early this century, a hybrid larch was produced, the result of a union between the Japanese and European species.

The Tay remains a richly-wooded valley. Some pioneer silviculture was conducted in a nursery at the Perthshire abbey of Coupar, the monks insisting that their tenants should "put the land to every improvement" by "building and fencing and planting trees, that is ashes, osiers, birch, willow and broom, with hawthorn fences and protection from them".

Into these woods, in the late 1830s, came capercaillie, the big grouse of the northern pine forests. This species had died out in Britain and its reintroduction was arranged by Breadalbane of Taymouth, an exceedingly rich man. He was said to be able to walk in a straight line for over 100 miles and remain on his own estates. The Marquis of Breadalbane introduced Victoria and Albert to the Highlands, entertaining them at Taymouth Castle, exciting in them the possibilities of having a holiday home in the Highlands. Their choice of home was Balmoral, in the valley of the Dee, a property they purchased from the Gordons.

The capercaillie, brought to Perthshire with Breadalbane's keen interest, had been captured in Sweden. Sir Thomas Fowell Buxton had written to a Quaker named Llewellyn Lloyd, who lived in that country, and Lloyd rewarded the peasants who captured him some capercaillie that remained alive and well. Buxton's gamekeeper, Larry Banville, collected the birds in Sweden and transported them to Scotland in a little over a fortnight, using sailing packet, steamboat and mule cart. In 1837, Scotland had only 13 cock and 13 hen capercaillie. The spread of this species was encouraged by further introductions and by the thickly-wooded nature of the valleys. A British sporting record was set up at Dunkeld in 1910 when 69 caper were slain by seven guns.

The gamekeeper I met in England remembered when the woods of Tay valley were driven and 47 capercallie destroyed. "You drive caper like driving pheasants," he explained. "A caper, like a blackcock, tends to fly high; the technique is to drive them to a gully and shoot them as they cross." The capercaillie is a big bird, strongly feathered. "You don't think it is flying nearly as fast as it is," said the gamekeeper. "Caper break out of a wood singly or in pairs. They don't pack like other grouse." He did not care much for the taste of the bird.

"Some people like to eat it. I don't. It's the worst flesh I've ever tasted." The first task with a dead caper was to rip out its crop, "or the whole bird will taste of pine needles. The crop's usually full of a dense mass of green needles and young shoots. We just sent the bodies direct to London or Paris. These were about the only places interested in having them!"

Dunkeld is a worth-while destination in itself for a naturalist. Here he is first aware of birds and beasts with the Highland flavour. There are Scottish crossbills in some of the woods. Red squirrels are descendants of animals brought from Scandinavia by a Duke of Atholl who was concerned because the native squirrels were scarce. Wild rabbits, introduced to this district early in the nineteenth century, contributed to the sporting facilities. At about the same time, the Dukes of Atholl—proud of their estates and interested in everything that grew there— took a scientific interest in the salmon of the Tay; they systematically tagged fish before this practice became common in research projects.

Some of the hollow trees by the river are the nesting place of goosanders. When the nesting season is over, and the moult is imminent, birds fly to quiet lochans on the hills. One of the areas chosen is the Loch of Lowes, the largest of three lochs lying close together. Loch of Lowes was the first reserve acquired by the Scottish Wildlife Trust.

It is a shallow loch, ringed by native trees—Scots pine, alder, birch. Queen Victoria, a visitor in 1865, pronounced it "very pretty". At about that time a pair of great-crested grebe delighted local naturalists by successfully rearing a family here. Loch of Lowes is one of the nesting places of the osprey. An observation hide was erected for visitors, who can watch the fish hawk hunting or perched at its tree-top nest.

The mammals include roe and also a dark-toned fallow deer, descendants of stock introduced by (inevitably) a Duke of Atholl. The wild cat is present. My gamekeeper friend had told me: "A wild cat's timid—unless it's been cornered. Then it can be very, very fierce. We used to find kits in rock cairns on the hills in spring—the time we went out looking for fox earths. The terriers killed any kits that stayed among the rocks. We shot any kits that bolted." The wild cat endures in a changing world; it benefits from the modern afforestation schemes which give it cover—and peace.

The road up Strathtay was one of the highways made by General Wade, who arrived in Scotland during the summer of 1724, held the king's commission as commander-in-chief for 15 years and, between 1725 and 1736, supervised the laying of 250 miles of metalled roads of an average width of 16 feet. Wade was one of those who opened up the Highlands. Of him it was written:

> Had you seen these roads before they were made;
> You would lift up your hands and bless General Wade.

His Great North Road is prosaically known as the A9 and passes through scenery on the grand scale. Near Dunkeld I scanned the river side and watched merganser, grey wagtail, oyster-catcher and ringed plover. In the evening I entered Pitlochry. The air had chilled. There was the promise of overnight frost.

The cold air encouraged me to swing my arms as I strode to the dam that is part of a hydro-electricity scheme. The lacklustre waters of Faskally, a man-made loch, looked steely blue, bordering on blackness. A trickle of pilgrims shuffled through an observation room connected to the fish pass, but few salmon were moving. Researchers have found that a dominant factor in the spring run is temperature, and salmon are not inclined to ascend until the water temperature reaches 41–49 degrees Fahrenheit. Human visitors, adults and small children, peered with equal enthusiasm through misty glass into one of the 35 pools of the pass by which salmon can reach Faskally and move up the river system to the spawning grounds. The pass, I discovered, has an ingenious counting device and can distinguish between fish on the spawning run and the kelts (spent fish) moving back downriver.

The world beyond the plate glass of the observation room was cold, silent, mysterious. Two salmon rested against the

current. Their journey, possibly begun in the deeps off Greenland, would reach fulfilment by courtesy of the hydro-electricity
board high up in the central hills of Scotland.

I slept fitfully and opened my eyes at 5 am. Walking stiffly
to the window, blinking sleep from my eyes, I saw that the tops
of the hills west of the Tay were banded by yellow sunlight.
Blobs of light mist were so still they might have been tethered to
the upper slopes. The river steamed. My car was encased in ice.

For a few hours I had Scotland to myself, travelling joyfully in
the spirit of the Reverend Thomas Grierson, a nineteenth-century
minister of Kirkbean, who tramped the Highlands and aimed to
cover 15 or 20 miles before breakfast. It was another servant of
the kirk, Kenneth Macleod, who in 1915 composed the song I
could not ignore when, turning left just north of Pitlochry, and
crossing a comparatively new bridge over the Garry, I thought
of some of the features immediately ahead:

> Sure, by Tummel and Loch Rannoch
> And Lochaber I will go,
> By heather tracks wi' heaven in their wiles;
> If it's thinkin' in your inner heart
> Braggart's in my step,
> You've never smelt the tangle o' the Isles.

To my left, well below road level, were the Tummel Falls—
or what remains of them following the coming of hydro-
electricity. When Loch Tummel was dammed, the water level
rose for 15 feet and an impressive reservoir was formed, but for
centuries before that the salmon had hurled themselves at the
falls, which they could only negotiate in wet periods when the
river was in spate. People caught salmon by attaching baskets
to the rocks, trapping some of the fish as they fell back after
unsuccessfully leaping.

An early start to the day enabled me to see the last of the
night shift in the animal world. A startled roebuck leapt from
the roadway just ahead of the car and bounced to a halt on
rough ground. We stared at each other. The only sounds were
the ticking of a loose tappet in the car engine and the whirr of

the heater as it slowly melted the remaining ice from the windows. The buck tripped into the cover of spruce with a flare of caudal white.

It was the first of several roe deer I was to observe in a chilly, pre-breakfast world. One roe was a young male, its antlers consisting of two upright prongs. A matronly doe paused between conifers in a dark part of a wood and could conceivably have kids to attend. May and June is the time for calving.

I had not travelled far before I was aware of the presence of the Forestry Commission, which has 20,000 acres in this area. On rising ground to my right, among the packed conifers, hen capercaillie would be brooding eggs. Or so I was to be assured by a forester. Where the pinewood world of the caper petered out at about 1,000 feet above sea level there are black grouse. Foresters tolerate the capercaillie up to a point, but generally detest the black grouse, which nip the terminal buds from young conifers, distorting the growth of the trees.

Beyond the Queen's View (of the Tummel) I expected more than even a benevolent Scotland could reasonably offer. The large bird perched on a boulder, its feathers burnished by strong sunlight, had to be a golden eagle! It was actually a cock pheasant which, I later heard, is an equally scarce bird by Tummel and Rannoch.

A tawny owl, surveying me from a perch on one of the overhead wires, rolled its head to keep the car in view. The bird's modest-sized neck was swaddled in feathers and could not be seen; it seemed that the head was revolving on ball-bearings!

The waders clamouring around waste land compensated me for not having time to visit the Dunalastair marshes, between Lochs Tummel and Rannoch. The compensatory throng included lapwings and the curlew, a bird known as the 'whaup' in old Scotland. A snipe used a boulder as a platform from which to give its *chipper, chipper* call, and another snipe made a series of shallow dives in the air. The wind rushed through extended outer tail feathers and the familiar bleating sound was heard, giving point to a Gaelic name for the snipe, *Gabhar-athair*, meaning 'goat of the air'. The sound is mechanical, not vocal.

Greylags are said to breed around Tummel. This ancestor of the domestic goose which provided flight feathers for the arrows of medieval armies and quills for many masters of literature— also for office clerks—has for long had a nesting stronghold in Scotland. Scottish birds were the ancestors of greylags which now nest in the English Lake District. I saw three adult greylags swimming surreptitiously near the edge of Tummel. No downy young birds were in sight, but they have been seen here.

Where Tummel ended with banks of sand and mud—for I saw it during a period of drought—Canada geese and a solitary pink-footed goose were engaged in finicky preening, probing and smoothing feathers with their bills, beating their wings and flicking their tails during their prolonged toilet. A female red-breasted merganser floated as still as a cork close to the bank; there was double beauty because it was almost perfectly reflected in the water. Doubtless it had already dined, diving for its fish food which would include *parr*, or young salmon. The mandibles of a merganser have serrations which enable it to maintain a firm grip on slimy fish scales, hence the bird's sub-title of 'sawbill'. Mergansers have been frequently destroyed by men with fishing interests. Little can be done with the body of the bird; the flesh is as appetising as an old car tyre!

The village of Kinloch Rannoch, viewed in the brilliant but early sunshine, was a ghost place. There was not even a plume of smoke from a chimney to hint at human occupation. During a brisk walk I stopped to survey the shapeliest of the local peaks, Schiehallion, which tickles the clouds at 3,547 feet. Its summit can be reached without much physical effort. Once a turf hut stood near the summit. Schiehallion was used as a station for important astronomical experiments, Dr Maskelyne, Astronomer Royal in the 1770s, applying himself by observation and experiment to determining the weight of planet Earth. Legends have been woven around the hill, and local people were terrorized by a mysterious beast—"a dog, a he-goat, a dark moving mass, or some other object, which, from the unaccountable manner of its appearance and disappearance, could not be deemed earthly".

Little more than a bowshot from Kinloch Rannoch lay Loch

Rannoch, which is nine and a half miles long, comparatively broad and devoid of islands. This morning it was calm, mirror-like and serene—in contrast to the nurseryland of some of the streams that feed it, for they emanate from wild Rannoch Moor, lying to the west.

A sandpiper tripped along the shore 50 yards from where I parked the car. I watched the bird 'teetering', moving its hinder part vigorously up and down as though determined to shake it off. The sandpiper flew, low over the loch, one moment beating its wings and the next gliding, wings down-curved, their tips almost trailing in the water.

A few years ago Rannoch became nationally famous as the name of a peregrine falcon. Found by a gamekeeper walking not far from the loch, the bird was adopted by the Royal Society for the Protection of Birds. In this area are some tree-nesting golden eagles. Red-throated divers frequent hill lochans. Sparrow-hawks and buzzards are relatively common, and an osprey has been seen prospecting the floodlands below the village.

Living in this area by the right of many thousands of generations is the wild cat, which is often talked about but rarely seen. A forester told me of a farmer crossing the hills and coming close to a wild cat as it sunned itself. He stood, watched the animal for a quarter of an hour and then whistled. The cat—a nocturnal hunter, always jittery in the daylight—sprang up and streaked away. The Scottish wild cat is not a domestic tabby gone wild but the local representative of a distinct species, with a tail handsomely barred, and manner fierce when it has been cornered. The wild cat is virtually untamable even at kittenhood. The kitten develops into a mini-tiger! Male cats have been known to kill their own young, which is one reason why a female sneaks away to drop her kits in seclusion.

Said a gamekeeper, as we chatted about the rich and varied animal life: "We don't have the pine marten. We fully expect to see it one day!"

The road near the loch, which meandered in an amiable sort of way, had not outgrown its status of a small country lane. The hard surface, and a capacious litter bin in a lay-by, were the only concessions to modernity. The road was patterned by the grey-blue shadows of many trees. Among them were Scots pine which had grown well beyond the pyramidical form of infancy; they had, indeed, become individuals. I was close to the Black Wood of Rannoch.

2

THE BLACK WOOD

A stranger to the Highlands, hearing about the Black Wood of
Rannoch, imagines that it lies in perpetual shadow or was
desolated by fire at a time when men were giving names to
topographical features. It stands on land that rises gently from
the shores of the loch and is not dominated by craggy hills. There
was a serious fire in Victorian times, but by then the name of
the wood was very old, and a Mr Wentworth promptly had the
devastated areas replanted with similar species of trees to those
destroyed.

Black Wood of Rannoch: the name has some sinister con-
notations. Yet no coven of witches met here, and the only illicit
activity I heard of was the distilling of whisky, a practice once
so general it became respectable. From timber in the Black Wood
of Rannoch came resin and turpentine.

A 'black wood' in Scotland is one containing pine trees. It
is a comparative term, distinguishing this type from an altogether
lighter deciduous wood. The darkest object I have found in the
Black Wood of Rannoch is the fruit of the blaeberry, and even
this had its lustrous blackness relieved by silver where the berry
caught the light. An old pinewood such as that at Rannoch can
glow warmly when it has caught the eye of the sun. There is
a golden hue on the upper branches of the most venerable trees
from which some of the outer bark has peeled, revealing the
reddish shade of the wood beneath. Some of the Scots pine are
300 years old, and one of them has a trunk rising straight

as a ship's mast for 80 feet before the canopy of foliage begins.

Heather is strong and luxuriant in the areas where Scots pine grows really well. Walk through the Black Wood of Rannoch in June and you detect a greenish hue where several common species of plant have put forth fresh leaves. Bracken unfurls, the fronds at first like bishops' croziers; they die back to contribute mightily to the rich tones of autumn. By then the heather has blossomed and reverted to its impassive dark appearance, and there has been a rich fruiting of berries, food for birds and beasts, as the purple droppings of capercaillie and fox testify at this time. In winter, the pine trees may look black, but that is only because the eyes have been seared by the brilliance of the snow that gives even the most sombre of pine woods a lightness and gaiety. During the lean months, capercaillie stuff themselves with a monotonous diet of pine needles, and *churring* bands of titmice poke in the crannies of the trees for oddments of food a human can scarcely see.

I went to the Black Wood of Rannoch to feel the kinship with a thousand or two generations of people who had preceded me to these wild parts. In a changing world, an old pine forest changes little. There is natural regeneration, and the rhythm is very slow in one of the Scottish remnants of the vast coniferous forest that stretched across northern Europe for thousands of miles. Here I could enjoy the world as it was about 8,000 years ago.

Whether or not the Black Wood of Rannoch and the other 'black woods' of the Highlands are entirely natural makes a point for lively discussion when foresters meet, for it is arguable that nothing has escaped the hand of man. In 1883, when the Black Wood formed part of the Dall estate, Thomas Hunter published a book on the woods, forests and estates of Perthshire. The owner at Rannock was Mr T. V. Wentworth, "an enthusiastic arboriculturalist" who reverenced the old wood.

Earlier that century, part of the Black Wood was desecrated by an English timber company. Pines were felled, the branches lopped off, and the trunks levered on to a mile-long chute leading to the shore of Loch Rannoch. Thomas Hunter was told that the trunks attained such a speed that they "stuck as fast as stakes in deep water, while the sheer weight of not a few caused them to sink to the bottom, never to rise again". The plan was to float logs down the Tay, intercepting them miles lower down. Many logs eluded the men and drifted into the North Sea, where they became a shipping hazard!

A forester told me with pride: "The Black Wood still stands. Everywhere else, man seems to have done his damnest to get rid of the old forests". He was exaggerating, of course, but the point was worth emphasizing. The few remains of the Caledonian pine forest are like green blotches on the map of Highland Scotland. Most of these relict areas are concentrated in the valley of the Spey.

The heyday of the Caledonian forest occurred long before man set foot on the scene. There are men today who cherish what bits remain, and among them is my forester friend at Rannoch. The Nature Conservancy is also concerned. The forests were intensively studied during the 1950s, and now the programme of research has been renewed by the Conservancy, which seeks to determine—and to describe in detail—the range of variation existing. It will be linked with environmental factors. Special note is being made of the occurrence of natural regeneration in the pine woods.

The story of the Caledonian forest began about 20,000 years ago. The last of the ice sheet was diminishing fast. The Pleistocene period was drawing to a close. The wind blew unchecked across tundra where, during the short, hot summers, reindeer browsed. Then trees broke into the bleakness of the tundra, and the first trees were Arctic birch and willow. Birch swept the scene and behind it came the pine. The so-called Scots pine is a local variant of pines that are far-spread across Europe.

Pines dominated the scene, but there were still many birch trees—as, indeed, there are today. An English forester tends to think of birch as a weed, and the English tourist in the Highlands marvels at its autumnal beauty. On days when there is just a puff of wind, the golden leaves shimmer in the crisp air. It has been so for a time incomprehensible to man.

Man was absent during the years when pines dominated the Highlands, filling the main valleys, extending up the side valleys, moving high up the hills. The forest regenerated itself in what has been described as the 'shift' of the pines. Trees advance up the slopes, thriving in the light. When trees in the areas behind them decay—or are obliterated, perhaps by some natural disaster such as fire induced by a lightning flash—the movement is reversed.

Among and on the pines lived a sparse but distinctive fauna. Nature was, roughly, in balance. There were brown bears in the forest. The size and temper of this animal made it a candidate for local extinction when man had moved in, but not until about the tenth century AD had the species been eliminated. The wild boar, smaller and more devious, endured for a little longer than the bear. The pure stock may have died out early in the sixteenth century; the blood, diluted somewhat by crossing, survived in the domestic swine of the Highlanders.

The elk lived in the Caledonian forest, and here too was the beaver, obsessed with water level and ceaselessly damming the streams before being phased out of Highland life centuries ago, but a number of distinctive bird species remain. Though it cannot easily be proved, the crested tit has presumably occupied the pine forest since Boreal times. It is now locally relatively scarce, though expanding its range by taking advantage of the new coniferous plantations. The miracle is that such a specialist bird—and one whose population is badly affected by the grimmest winters—should have survived at all in tight little Britain.

We last considered the Caledonian forest in its heyday. Gradually, the weather became moist, though it remained warm. What is now Britain was tethered to the mainland of Europe by a land bridge across which there was a slow but grand procession of trees and their attendant animal life. A sinking landscape meant the end of the land bridge. The few species of trees already in Britain could not now be augmented by other species, for Britain was now an off-shore island. European larch, which was

Young hen capercaillie of a species well represented in the
Central Highlands

The curlew—known in Scotland as whaup—nesting in a meadow
A cock lapwing takes its turn in the incubation of eggs

introduced by man in comparatively recent times, would normally have reached us without man's help. The Norway spruce, now a popular Christmas tree, had possibly been swept from Britain by advancing ice; we had become an island before it could return naturally. The Norway spruce was reintroduced in modern times.

There was a brief return to dry conditions, and the pines rallied, but then the climate became wet and cold. Marshland and swamps formed in the bottoms of the glens, and peat was thickly deposited on the hills. Broad-leaved trees liked the new conditions, oak—for instance—being able to extend its range far into Scotland.

The pine forest was now restricted to a few favourable areas, mainly in the central and north-eastern parts of the Highlands, which remain much drier than the west. Pines stayed rooted in the glacial drifts of Strathspey, which for centuries remained an inaccesible area. The rate and degree of deforestation in southern Scotland were staggering, most of the woodland having been cleared by the twelfth century. A tight-lipped Scottish Parliament of 1503 heard that the woods of Scotland had been "utterly destroyed", but the members in 1609 rejoiced at the discovery of "certane wodis in the heylandis".

Landowners from about the middle of the eighteenth century planted millions of trees; lumbermen operating during the two world wars felled on a massive scale. Canadian lumbermen strode through the Black Wood of Rannoch. The owner, realizing the uniqueness of what remained, made it possible for the Forestry Commission to take over this area, and the Commission preserves the finest stretches with little human interference.

As I walked up a rough track between old pines, I occasionally looked behind, noticing that my boots left clear impressions in dark, moist peat. I felt relaxed, at ease, with so much natural beauty around me. The pines were widely spaced, attended by junipers, some birch and rowan. Sir T. B. Lauder, writing of "fir woods" in Deeside, noticed that there was no tiresome uniformity in what remains of the Caledonian forest:

c

Every movement we make exposes to our view fresh objects
of excitement and discloses new scenes produced by the
infinite variety of the surface. At one time we find ourselves
wandering along some natural level under the deep and sublime
shade of the heavy Pine foliage, upheld high overhead by the
tall and massive columnar stems, which appear to form an
endless colonnade; the ground dry as the floor beneath our
footsteps, the very sound of which is muffled by the thick
deposition of decayed Pines with which the seasons of more
than one century have strewed it; hardly conscious that the sun
is up, save from the fragrant resinous odour which its influence
is exhaling, and the continuous hum of the clouds of insects that
are dancing in its beams over the tops of the trees.

Lauder wrote of the summer forest, the time when it has an
aromatic tang that only those suffering from the common cold
will miss. At one point in my walk I detected the faint and
dying scent of a fox. Chaffinches called; they are probably the
commonest of the forest birds. There were willow warblers,
which have been in sweet springtime song in these parts since
life became tolerable after the Ice Ages. A robin eyed me from
a pine. A wren scuttered close to the ground. A mistle thrush
departed, chattering harshly.

When I was not questing for birds, I watched ant traffic on
the path where it levelled out and I found ant heaps untouched
by man or woodpeckers. One ant was carrying a piece of
vegetation which, scaled up to an equivalent load for a human,
would have been a telegraph pole. I felt that I was beholding
a routine of behaviour half as old as the world.

A capercaillie took me by surprise. It was a cock bird, already
in noisy, headlong flight when I became aware of it. Had the
bird been questing for ants? A gamekeeper I was to meet on
Speyside told me that young capers are fond of ants. He found
a deserted nest. Not only had the caper eggs become cold, but
they had actually sunk into the nesting material. He believed
the bird that had been brooding them was taken by a fox. The
gamekeeper returned home with the eggs and he hatched them
out under a broody hen. He then spent part of each day trans-

porting buckets full of ant eggs from a local wood to the pen in which the young capers were living until they became independent enough to be released.

The capercaillie is tolerated by a forester—up to a point. This bird is undoubtedly a potential menace in woodland. Johnstone considered 76 naturally-regenerated and 89 planted trees in the Black Wood of Rannoch and discovered that capercaillie had taken the leader from 44 per cent of the planted trees but from only 14 per cent of the trees that had been naturally regenerated. It is assumed that the capercaillie finds more nutrition in planted trees.

The road beyond the Black Wood peters out at the edge of Rannoch Moor, the last flourish of civilization being a railway station. A fortunate visitor sees a golden eagle soaring on the thermals. There is some consolation, in the absence of the real thing, in contemplating the stone eagles set on the gateposts leading to the former Army barracks at Rannoch. The government billeted soldiers here early in the eighteenth century when —as one local writer observed—Rannoch was "in an uncivilized barbarous state, under no check, or restraint of laws". Soldiers laid hands on a thief and promptly hanged him at his own door. The barbarism of the local population ended with this equally barbarous act by the military.

The Reverend Duncan McAra, minister of the parish of Fortingall during the latter part of the eighteenth century, mentioned "swarms of tinkers, sailors and vagrants from the great towns who, by dreadful imprecations and threatenings, extort charity, and immediately waste it in drunkenness and riot".

I returned to Kinloch Rannoch having seen one person!

3

ROAD TO SPEYSIDE

By the middle of the eighteenth century, there were no wolves in Scotland. Packs of wolves had preyed on the deer herds, invariably killing the weakest, and there was no longer a predator so strong and fleet-footed it could pull down a mature deer. For years men had hunted deer with hounds, but little more than 50 years after the last wolf was slain even this traditional practice had ended. The last deer hunt in the old style is said to have taken place at Atholl in 1800.

These thoughts came to me, of all places, at the point where the Great North Road was being radically improved and traffic lights were in operation holding up the flow of traffic. I had entered the wooded gorge of Killicrankie, a few miles north of Pitlochry, where Sir Ewen Cameron of Lochiel destroyed the last local wolf in 1680. We do not know the circumstances. Much better documented is the story of the slaying of the last wolf in Strathspey. It was walloped by a gridiron wielded by Big Sally of Duthil!

Highlanders did not stop at killing wolves. A carnage of astonishing proportions took place early in the nineteenth century, when landowners embarked on game-rearing schemes. They tried to eliminate the natural predators. When Colonel Thornton came through Glen Garry towards the end of the eighteenth century, he would take the richness of the wild life for granted. Between 1837 and 1840, the preservers of game destroyed 198 wild cats, 246 pine martens, 106 polecats, 98 peregrine falcons, 78 merlins, 15 golden eagles, 27 white-tailed eagles, 18 ospreys, 63 goshawks, 275 kites, 475 ravens and 1,431 hooded crows. There were other creatures on the list!

Nature has been sadly unbalanced ever since, though the Dukes of Atholl introduced some birds and beasts, mainly of a sporting character. Their home, Blair Castle, was referred to as "one of the most splendid hunting chateaux in Europe". In the mid-nineteenth century when they possessed 194,640 acres and drew £40,768 in rents, they could look back on many vivid incidents in the family saga, not least the visit of Mary Queen of Scots who "derived no ordinary pleasure" from a hunt arranged for her. The modern mind boggles at the scale of the hunt which took place in the sixteenth century. Clansmen numbering 2,000 drove game from Atholl, Badenoch, Mar and Moray. As the beasts of the chase began to converge on each other, wolves were running with the deer. Five wolves and 360 deer were reported slain.

Colonel Thornton wrote about seeing "a true Highland greyhound, which is now become very scarce". He was referring to the animal used by the chieftains when stag-chases were arranged. The Colonel referred to Mr Pennant's tour and this traveller's record of a dog he had seen—"the offspring of a wolf and Pomeranian bitch. It had much the appearance of the first, and was very good-natured and sportive; but, being slipped at a weak deer, it instantly brought the animal down, and tore out its throat."

Beyond Blair Atholl, the road has a rising gradient. It is nowhere conspicuously steep, gaining altitude with the greatest consideration for traffic. I was approaching the Pass of Drumochter, in the type of Highland country Dr Johnson may have had in mind when he wrote:

> An eye accustomed to flowery pastures and waving harvests is astonished and repelled by this wide extent of hopeless sterility. The appearance is that of matter incapable of form or usefulness, dismissed by Nature from her case and disinherited of her favours, left in its original elemental state, or quickened only with one sullen power of useless vegetation.

On reflection, it is unfair to apply this to Drumochter. Most writers refer to its bleakness, but this does not necessarily mean dreariness. The stretch where the Great North Road runs between high hills can be powerfully dramatic when the mist is down and there is a sullen, brooding moorland. I had been this way in early August, just before the flowering of the ling, when the 'dreary' slopes were patchy with flowering bell-heather, against whose beauty the more widespread purple of ling would look downright vulgar.

Colonel Thornton remembered Drumochter mainly because of his attempt to transfer live perch over the watershed. He hoped to stock some of the Badenoch lochs, in which no perch had been seen. With perch in mind, the Colonel had brought a tin kettle all the way from London. He planned to fill the kettle, drop in some perch, then keep the fish alive by replenishing the kettle with fresh water at every burn he saw.

The road was rough. At every jolt of the gig, the kettle spilled some of its water. The Colonel thought of hiring a man to carry it on foot for the next 10 miles, but local men wanted eight days' wages for less than one day's fairly easy work. After crossing Drumochter, the Colonel plunged the almost empty kettle into the river at Dalwhinnie, and the perch began to revive. He then persuaded a soldier to carry the kettle to Raits, his Highland headquarters, but the soldier eventually turned up with half-dead fish that never recovered.

Drumochter is from *Druim Uachdar,* meaning 'ridge of the upper ground'. River, railway, road, telegraph wires and electric power lines run side by side, breasting the summit at about 1,500 feet above sea level. Over the line of the pass, towards the end of October, fly skeins of grey geese on migration from their far northern breeding grounds to the benevolent fields of southern Scotland. The average size of a skein is between 20 and 60 birds, yet parties of about 150 birds have been recorded.

Usually the geese pass over Speyside at more than 1,000 feet. The sight of the wavering chevrons and the gabbling of the birds excites even the local people, while implying that winter—often a bitterly cold season in Strathspey—is imminent. When there is unsettled weather, the migrating geese descend to low altitudes where they believe they are safe. They have been seen passing over tree-clad hills near Newtonmore at little more than the height of the conifers.

Few geese are observed passing over the valley of the Spey in April and May, the time of the northward migration. (A number of geese may spend part of the winter in the area.) It is assumed through a paucity of reports that birds going north with the spring take a more westerly course.

Drumochter, this great pass between steep hills that lie almost halfway between the west and east coasts of Scotland, sees the passage of other bird migrants in autumn. They deserve greater study at this natural funnel. This way come flocks of Scandinavian and north European thrushes, the fieldfares and redwings which, after crossing the North Sea, make a landfall on the Moray Firth and take a southward course through Speyside. Rowan trees on the hillsides are flaring with scarlet berries as the Grampian ring-ouzels depart for their wintering areas, which are mainly on the Atlas Mountains of North Africa.

While crossing Drumochter, I was delayed by road work. General George Wade set the line of the road. He had his critics. A Victorian chief inspector of roads took him to task for piling the excavated material on either side of the road, leaving what was virtually a wide ditch. "No great inconvenience was occasioned by this mode of construction in Summer; but in Winter it evidently formed a complete receptacle for snow."

I was in Macpherson country. The clan lands extended 15 miles west of Kingussie to Loch Killin, north-east to the Cairngorms and south to Dail-na-mine Forest. The Macphersons took as their crest a wild cat. Drumochter Lodge stood sedately within a circlet of trees. It had a French look, with corner turrets, and the walls had been whitened.

The area known as Badenoch was entered under the glowering stare of the Boar of Badenoch (2,422 feet) and the equally stern Sow of Atholl, a slightly lesser peak. The Garry ended with marshland tenanted by redshank and wigeon. The streams now ran northwards, towards the Spey. Somewhere on Drumochter,

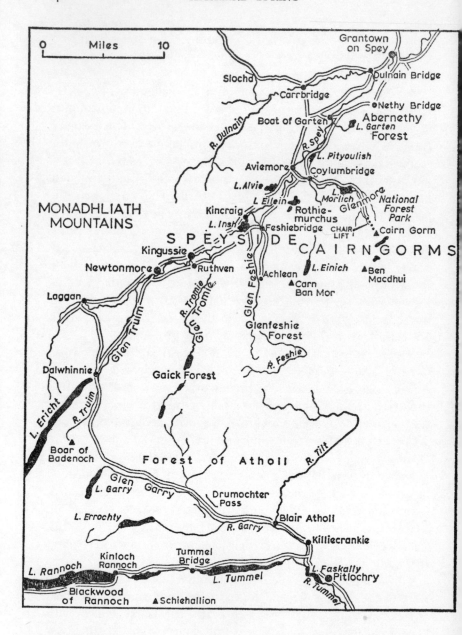

the Truim had risen and would give the Spey its first important transfusion of fresh water at a point near Newtonmore. Badenoch looked forbidding, sombre. The forest of Gaick, away to my right, was so wild and boggy that some people who ventured there were lost or injured. Five men who hunted hinds in Gaick Forest in the winter of 1799 spent the night in a bothy and did not awake; an avalanche of snow roared down and overwhelmed their shelter.

Soon I was in a part of Glen Truim where the roadside was gay with birch trees. Were there redwings nesting here? The species has now spread down to Perthshire. Eight miles north-wards from Drumochter, I came close to—but remained out of sight of—Loch Ericht, 'loch of meetings', now dramatically terminated by a dam. Man has tamed and now controls the loch, but he has made little mark on Ben Alder, the dominating hill, where the dotterel has nested in the glare of summer snow.

Professor W. H. Pearsall, in his important work on Highland Britain, commented on a geographical dividing line in these parts. Sometimes, when the Cairngorms stand out cloudlessly, or with small fair-weather clouds, the big western bens are sunk in mist or dwarfed by rainclouds. Pearsall suggested that the contrast was most noticeable about a line drawn north and south through the Loch Ericht or Dalwhinnie.

The high grassy hills west of the Spey are not exactly despised —they are virtually ignored by those who look for a first viewing of the Cairngorms. Yet the Monadhliath are equally interesting. Here nests the ptarmigan, and in October flocks of from 100 to 150 birds have been seen. Contributing to the spring chorus is the dunlin, a bird which gives the impression of being matey but is a master at drawing human attention from its nest. The dunlin rises well in advance of an intruder's arrival. Flying for 30 or 40 feet, it pitches down into the heather—and keeps a watching brief. Hamish Marshall, of Grantown, was trudging on these heights during the first week in May when he had considerable luck, finding three dunlin nests in less than an hour. He is a most experienced hill-walker, but had never found the nest of this species before.

The Great North Road, with its heavy, purposeful traffic, was becoming oppressive. Leaving it at Dalwhinnie, I drove towards Laggan. There was a time when travellers used this road to reach the Great Glen, crossing Corrieyairack Pass on a road constructed at the orders of General George Wade; it descended to Ford Augustus. Regular travellers found that snow lay on Corrieyairack for months on end, and three lairds recommended that a route at a lower level should be made to replace "the present one by Garvamore over Corry Arrick, which from its height is at all times dangerous and generally impossible for four months in the year, to the prejudice of His Majesty's service and the loss of the lives of many of his soldiers and subjects".

A new route extended from Spean Bridge, by Loch Laggan to Kingussie. Cattle drovers had used the Corrieyairack route, with its impressive hairpins, long before military necessity prompted the building of a serviceable road. And when ordinary travellers were joyously using the new low route, the cattle drovers continued to come over Corrieyairack. Some of them stayed at the Garvamore inn, resting their shaggy black beasts during a long trek to the trysts at Falkirk and Crieff.

Near Dalwhinnie I had my first hint of the presence of red deer, tall fencing having been set up against the road. I heard from a local man of some of the problems affecting estates with deer on their land. In recent time there has been a loss of deer wintering ground. Good stags were being shot as marauders in winter. Poaching was undertaken by men who had the high mobility provided by cars, and some good roads on which to speed away with the carcasses of animals they had slain. Each estate devised and ran its own policy until 1970, when the Monadhliath Deer Group was formed. Now the various aspects of deer management are dealt with by a consortium of proprietors.

In 1801 the wife of the parish minister at Laggan was a Mrs Grant. She wrote *Letters from the Mountains*, the reading of which added a welcome touch of fantasy to the experiences of my journey. Mrs Grant described "the fairy mounds, or little

regularly-formed cones, which abound so much in the highlands". They had been accounted the residence of fairies. "In
some places, as at the foot of the mountain Corryarick, on the
south side, a large space of ground is entirely covered with them.
These are most regularly formed of equal size, and covered with
the bilberry and foxglove. . . . All along that road, numbers of
these conical hillocks are seen rising in dry, gravelly ground, and
thickly covered with heath."

A Badenoch worthy told her of venturing near the foot of
Corrieyairack, hearing the sound of fairies turning their bread
on the girdle "and finding the smell of the oatcakes they were
toasting waken appetite very forcibly". Listening to his stories,
Mrs Grant was delighted but sceptical. He was the only person
she ever knew who "admitted to so near a cognisance of the
domestic economy of these fantastic sprites; and, to say truth,
his own friends were wont to smile at his details with com-
placent, but suspicious, silence".

Newtonmore has, to an Englishman, a refreshingly straight-
forward name. I asked a man at this "new town on the moor"
if he could tell me about the location of golden eagles. Scotland
has an estimated 200 breeding pairs, and I was anxious to see at
least one bird.

The man glared suspiciously—as well he might, knowing that
in the past strangers have ransacked many eyries—but then his
native hospitality asserted itself. He told me that eagles nest
"about 12 miles away", waving his arms to indicate—in the
most general terms—the hill ranges to the east. A gamekeeper
was equally guarded. He had seen an eagle at an unnamed place
10 hours walking distance into the Monadhliath! I was welcome
to look for the eyrie on this enormous block of upland extending
between Speyside and the Great Glen. On the grassy, now partly
forested, Monadhliath are the sources of three notable Highland
rivers: Nairn, Findhorn and Spey.

The new forests have a commercial purpose, and little of the
natural woodland remains. The Stuart brothers, in *Lays of the
Deer Forest*, wrote nostalgically of the forest of Darnaway, on
the middle course of the Findhorn:

Few know what Darnaway was in those days—almost untrodden except by the deer, the roe, the foxes, and the pine martens, its green dells filled with lilies of the valley, its banks covered with wild hyacinths, primroses and pyrolas, and its deep thickets clothed with every species of woodland luxuriance, the blossoms, grass, moss, and timber of every kind, growing with the magnificence and solitude of an aboriginal wilderness, a world of unknown beauty and silent loneliness, broken only by the sough of the pines, the hum of the water, the hoarse bell of the buck, the long wild cry of the fox, the shriek of the heron or the strange, mysterious tap of the northern woodpecker. For ten years we knew every dell and bank and thicket.

For miles I had been conscious that after the long drag from Blair Atholl the burns and rivers I saw were flowing northwards, but I cannot recall precisely just where I became aware of the Spey. This river spends its early life in the wilds of Corrie-yairack. A lively flow of water enters Loch Spey, and from here to Loch Insh, near Kingussie, is a distance of about 40 miles. The river has another 60 miles to flow before it is stung by salt about Garmouth.

Spey is a swift river—"swift above them all", proclaimed Timothy Pont, of Dunnet, in 1550. Spey is comparatively young as rivers go, still settling down and finding the most acceptable gradients after the chaos of the Ice Ages. Spey is a greedy river, and some odd geological chances have enabled it to draw water that might reasonably have gone into other systems—the Dee, for instance.

Spey has drawn considerable pride from local people, some of whom used to chant:

> The three largest rivers there be
> Are the Tay, the Spey and the Dee.

A Speyside superstition that invested the river with human qualities claimed that the river required to take one human life a year. Some other Highland watercourses were greedier in this respect!

I drove into Kingussie, passing the church dedicated to St

Columba. I also observed some young pine trees, which were appropriate to the place. Kingussie was *Ceann-a-ghuibhsaich*, the head of the fir forest. The Scots pine, once referred to as 'fir', is rendered in Gaelic *guis* or *guithais*. The forest declined, for a variety of reasons. For instance, in 1760 it was reported that people were cutting the hearts from the finest trees to serve as Candle-fir, "by which the Three [tree] perished, and decayed upon the Foot".

I liked Kingussie. It is a tidy town, little more than two long rows of well-built dwellings, shops and hotels extending along the main road. It was not always so attractive, unless you are a lover of rude simplicity. Elizabeth Grant, returning to Rothie-murchus from London in 1812, passed through the town and saw "a few very untidy-looking slated stone houses each side of the road". She noticed "bare heather on each side of the Spey, the bare mountains on each side of the heath, a few white-walled houses here and there, a good many black turf huts, frightful without, though warm and comfortable within. . . ."

The primitive simplicity of some old Highland dwellings could be appreciated at the Highland folk museum, tucked away at the end of a quiet street. Here was a thatched building that sheltered both people and stock; its interior was fragrant with peat. After I had walked through a room whose floor was strewn with rushes that smelled sweetly, the attendant mentioned that to the rushes had been added sweet herbs—wild thyme, bog myrtle, mint—that not only imparted fragrance but, especially the bog myrtle, discouraged flies and mice.

Colonel Thornton, attending the church late in the eighteenth century, had the impression that the men of Kingussie were there to eat tobacco, the women to sleep. "I may venture to affirm that a tax on sleeping females at church would bring in from this parish a pretty revenue."

Kingussie is the old capital of Badenoch. The name Badenoch is said to mean 'drowned lands'. Below Kingussie there is a sogginess about the valley of the Spey that may upset sufferers from rheumatism but delights the naturalist, who makes a com-pulsory halt at Loch Insh. At floodtime, there appears to be an inland sea between Kingussie and Loch Insh. The Spey, swollen by melt-water from the great snowfields of the Cairngorms and attended ranges, spills over the marshy flatlands. At Loch Insh itself, water cuts round and across a promontory, which becomes an island—the feature from which the loch is said to be named, Insh or *innis* meaning an island.

Spey in floodtime has overawed many writers. In the seventeenth century it was written: "Oftimes, this river in tyme of speat or stormie weather will be as bigg as if it were a logh, and also as broad, and overflows all the low corne lands of the country next to itself". The typical Highland loch is clear, cold, having little life, but shallow Loch Insh, edged with *equisetum*, is rich in all manner of creatures. Near Loch Insh is a mass of buckbean, which is known in England as bogbean.

I reached it at a time when the waterfowl were nesting. Some weeks before, local people had seen herds of bugling whooper swans departing for their northland nesting grounds, which they reach early in April. Now there were common terns in passage and about 30 goosander drakes. The ducks were presumably covering clutches of eggs in hollow trees not far from the burns.

A goosander duck that has not been disturbed might return year after year to the same tree hole, which occasionally is as low down as 2 feet 6 inches from the ground. From it, when they are one or two days old, the ducklings emerge, scrambling to the hole's rim with the assistance of claws attached to their webbed feet. Tumbling to the ground, the ducklings dutifully take up station behind the duck, and she leads them to water. By this time the debonair drake is one of a moulting group of birds.

A Highland bird photographer who had fumed and fretted near a goosander nest because the returning duck flew straight into the hole instead of alighting at the edge and posing for him, fixed some fine netting to the entrance. The returning duck checked her speed with incredible swiftness on seeing the wire, perching long enough for him to record the incident. Most bird photographers would not have approved of his technique.

Fishermen fume because, as one of them explained, "a goosan-

der can make a mess of the fishing". Hamish Marshall, of
Grantown, was standing quietly near the Spey one April
morning when a goosander alighted at a pool and began to fish.
He timed the bird. In 10 minutes precisely, 11 fish had been
caught. The duck lost only one of them which managed to
wriggle from the saw-toothed bill.

Modern tourists take the roads and bridges for granted. These
might almost have been laid down just after the Flood as part
of the Almighty's grand plan for the Highlands! Up to 1879,
the outflow of Loch Insh had no bridge, and travellers must use
a ferryboat.

One of the dry spots in the 'sponge of Badenoch' is a mound
at Ruthven which was a natural site for a castle. Here lived
the Wolf of Badenoch, Alexander Stewart, wild son of Robert II
who was appointed to the lordship of this area in 1371. The
Wolf was apparently a coarse man—a thug, indeed. He maintained a private army and terrorized the folk of the valley. When
there was a dispute between the Wolf and the Bishop of Moray
about some churchlands, the Wolf defied the cleric and even
set fire to the cathedral at Elgin.

The castle of the Wolf at Ruthven was seized and destroyed
by the rebel Earl of Ross in 1451, but the sixth Earl of Huntly
rebuilt it and here, in 1563, Queen Mary was entertained when
she came to Badenoch to hunt the deer. The present buildings
on the mound above the flood-plain were built as barracks in
the early part of the eighteenth century. In 1745, Ruthven was
called a "Redoubt".

I travelled on to Aviemore, seeing many features about which
the Colonel commented:

> the road pleasing and differing from all the Highland ones,
> not in the least hilly. . . . On the right you have immense hills;
> in the centre of the valley runs the noble, winding, rapid Spey,
> having innumerable coppices of birch on its banks. The opposite
> hills are covered, almost to the very skies, with immense forests
> of firs, and Glenmore and Rothemurcos woods, seven or eight
> miles broad, and twelve or fourteen long, give a melancholy shade
> to the pearl-coloured mountains around them.

The buzzard has returned in strength to the well-wooded floor of Strathspey. This was a breeding bird of the woods until game preservers drove it to remote crag sites. The fairly recent relaxation of keepering, and increasing awareness of the role of birds of prey in the natural world, have allowed it to return to the woods again. It has been estimated that over 30 pairs nest between Kingussie and Boat of Garten.

Stone circles near Aviemore testify to the one-time presence of Early Man. In modern times there was little more than an inn, a stopping place on the way to Inverness. By the middle of the nineteenth century a village of sorts had developed around a railway station. Thirty years ago it was not much more pretentious than a mid-West staging post. Now it resembles a city of the future—gleaming white, with hotels and various sports facilities. Yet siskins still sing from the birches in the shadow of Craigellachie, and on this towering crag, which thoroughly dominates Aviemore, is the eyrie of peregrine falcons. I saw a tiercel flashing by on scimitar-shaped wings.

From the platform of Aviemore station, where black-headed gulls swirl around each arriving train, the northern part of the Cairngorm range can be taken in at a glance. Mr Mikel Utsi, a rail passenger of some years ago, took a lingering glance at the Cairngorm slopes, diagnosed reindeer country and determined to bring some of these animals to the area, as I shall relate later.

Long before the toot of a railway locomotive was heard in Strathspey, Colonel Thornton took the road from here to Grantown. The modern road is silky smooth, but he traversed "a dreary moor", finding the road "encumbered by some exceeding large stones, or fragments of rocks in the centre, which ought to be blown up, being extremely dangerous at night to the traveller". Three miles from Grantown "the scene becomes more interesting, from the magnificence of the large woods, chequered with hanging banks of birch".

Once there was an old village, Freuchie, that had developed haphazardly. Then the Grants sought to enhance the beauty of their estate by clearing away the jumble of the years. On a tract of moorland they established a new town, Grantown, and here

I brought my dusty car to rest, while gentlefolk, sitting over afternoon tea at the hotels, doubtless talked about the Speyside of yesterday and, perhaps, commented on the supposed brashness of modern Aviemore.

Grantown, one of the 'new towns' of the eighteenth century, was first described in a notice of 1765, when interest in the project was being created. The site was in "a good pleasant country lying near plenty of Moss and other Firing . . . and a fine Limestone quarry, easily wrought . . . the Woods lying near, and to be had at low prices, and at very moderate charge floated down the Spey to Garmouth, where shipping may be easily had".

This was the point at which I became aware that the Spey valley was becoming softer, gentler, of greater value to farming —a countryside of golden grain and steaming distilleries that developed from the distillation plants kept at small farms and crofts so that families could supplement their income from farming. The 'hot' liquor was sold, the 'draff'—or what remained of the barley after distillation—being fed to the stock.

Heavy duties on home-made spirits debased the quality and raised the price, observed William Larkin in 1818. People took to distilling illegally, moving the liquor about the countryside deviously. "The smuggling of whisky is the only resource for the regular payment of their rents . . . the superiority of the smuggled article is so palpable that the demand for it is universal." When the large distilleries were developed there was an outcry from anglers as 'burnt ale' was discharged into the Spey, killing young salmon and sickening the adult fish. The Countess of Seafield led a representation of the Spey proprietors who, after a long legal battle, had the distillery owners restrained as to what they released into the river.

It amused me to discover that in the old days the upper classses tended to buy wine. Whisky was a coarse drink, fit only for the lower orders, and the common man preferred ale, which was cheap—twopence a Scottish pint, the equal of two English pints!

There is a wholesomeness about the distillation process as conducted in the Spey valley today. I visited a distillery, passing a pool of the purest water, listening to a Scottish tune ringing

D

out on bells in the clock tower. I went inside the range of buildings with a party of tourists, passing vats containing the 'porridge' and the 'mash', seeing the yeast being added, hearing about the long refining process, and standing amazed before the tall stills of burnished copper. There were three stills, side by side, looking like inverted mushrooms. When whisky has been distilled it is clear, the subtle colouring being derived from the sherry or oak casks in which it matures for seven and more years. These casks are bought fairly cheaply from the firms importing wine.

Grantown has a slice of primeval Scotland in its front garden. Between the houses and the Spey lie airy pine woods, carpeted with flowering plants such as blaeberry. They are not gloomy, but retain an air of mystery. The imaginative visitor could picture himself in the old Wood of Caledon. I strode here in the evening, listening for crossbills. The cock crossbill is uniquely coloured for a British bird, wearing Guardsman's red. The mandibles of this noisy little bird are uniquely formed, being crossed, like the twisted nib of a fountain pen. Spending most of its time in the woods of pine and larch, though occasionally wandering away from them (birds have been seen in Aviemore), the crossbills are among the exotic birds of Strathspey.

I neither saw nor heard crossbills here, though a local naturalist assured me they are present. Golfers at Grantown— who must often seek lost balls in the wood—have reported hearing the species all the year round. Crossbills are not particularly shy, but they are not numerous, being inconspicuous when set against the bottle-green crowns of the Scots pines.

The birds' feeding habits are curious. Often they are seen hanging upside down, like small parrots, neatly extricating seeds from the biggest cones, using the dexterity of their crossed mandibles and also a horny tongue. With small cones, the invariable practice is for a bird to nip off a cone and carry it to a nearby branch top, where it can be tackled more efficiently, held in a vice formed of branch and bird's foot. The debris trickles to the ground. Hamish Marshall of Grantown stayed in a cottage which had an iron roof. Crossbills ransacked the green pine cones immediately above, and the debris of cones fell on the iron roof with special clarity!

At what the countryfolk in my native Yorkshire call 'the edge o' dark', I was transported back to the days of the Picti, the 'tattooed folk'. A small van was being driven up the main street of Grantown, and everyone noticed it because from it came the sound of a handbell. Two men were sitting at the back of the van and they could be clearly seen because both doors were ajar. One of the men wore shorts—and nothing else except a smearing of a black substance. The van passed into the gloom; the sound of the handbell stopped.

A lady at the boarding house told me I had observed a 'blackening'. The young man who had been plastered with black was to be married on the following Saturday. "He wears nothing but a wee pair o' pants. Then they darken him with soot, oil, treacle, mixed up with a few feathers, and take him round the pubs. The bell is rung so that everyone knows about it. In the old days, it was supposed to be lucky to be blackened with soot."

This woman was a native of Grantown. She had some lively tales of local poachers. They sneaked back into town with salmon and the turkey-sized capercaillie. "My people liked the salmon, but they never did get used to caper. It's got a wild, piny flavour. The old people made it sweeter by burying the bird, feathers an' all, for a week. Or they'd slice open its crop and put in an onion before they cooked it." Palates must have been tougher in the sixteenth century, when Bishop Leslie wrote that the flesh of a capercaillie has "a gentle taste"!

When her last tale about poachers was told, it was nearly midnight. I went to bed in a cold room. A grey dawn followed.

4

PINES OF ABERNETHY

I went to Abernethy to see the Scottish crested tit, a diminutive bird which has its headquarters in the Spey valley. A middle-aged lady tending a garden in Nethy Bridge told me that she often saw crested tits in hard winters. They joined other titmice at the village bird tables, and did not allow larger birds to bully them, facing up to the blue or coal tit with arched backs and enraged calls. Some tits attacked peanuts with gusto, but the crested tit preferred the lumps of suet hung out in gardens by thoughtful local people. A gamekeeper had told her that when he left the carcass of a red deer outside his forest home in January—a time when there were no flies to be attracted to it—he saw crested tits flying into the rib cage to feed on fat.

The lady at Nethy Bridge did not think I would see the crested tit in the village. "The wee birds are in the woods, nesting." It had been a mild winter, and the nesting routine would possibly have begun a little earlier than usual.

A few hundred yards from the last dwelling in Nethy Bridge lay the first indigenous Scots pines of Abernethy. For a time I ceased to think about crested tits in my contemplation of this Highland forest. In modern pine plantations, the trees are so close together there is perennial gloom and the risk, if you enter, of having the clothes torn from your back. The ground, deprived of sunlight, has few green patches. The rest is a dull brown from a sterilizing mat of old needles. Few birds sing.

Abernethy and its neighbours, forming a great arc of bottle

green close up to the northern and western buttresses of the Cairngorms, are different. There are many new plantations, the young trees standing cheek-by-jowl like green-clad troops drawn up on parade, but you quickly forget them through the enchantment of the old-style wood. Here the pines are generously spaced, sending roots deep into the glacial deposits. Their waist-high companions are junipers, forming a thin scrub layer and offering many nesting sites for goldcrests. Far from being bare, the ground is covered by tall, stemmy plants—a mini-wood within a forest —of which ling, blaeberry and cowberry are easily recognized. The old pine forest is breezy, aromatic, tonally rich.

I did not motor in Abernethy because I lacked the energy to walk. By using the car as a hide I might see some of the shy forest creatures. It was quite early in the day, and roe deer crossing the track stood out conspicuously against grey grit; stuff that attracts the capercaillie. These birds use grit in their crops to help them digest a coarse, dry forest food, the winter fare of a capercaillie consisting mainly of needles plucked in tufts from the pine branches. Is there anything less appetising?

A young roebuck tripped across the forest road 20 yards ahead of the car. Was it curiosity or simply lack of fear in the presence of a car that impelled it to stand and watch? We eyed each other for five minutes, during which time the buck did not appear to move an inch. The simple spikes that were its antlers did nothing to focus attention as the widespread horn of larger species would have done. The deer was just a patch of light grey against the slightly darker grey of a forest not yet brightened by the sun.

When the sun did send rays slanting between the trees of Abernethy, the bark on the upper trunks and branches glowed redly and there was a heightened beauty in the canopy of dark green needles which, in the Scots pine, are arranged in pairs. The old warriors among the pines had an array of various ages of cones: old cones, now sprung, their seeds sent forth into the forest or eaten by squirrel and crossbill; brown cones that had been the fruit of the following year; green cones and those of the current year in the course of formation.

The pines of Abernethy, Glen More, Rothiemurchus and Glen Feshie endure not only because they stand on appropriate soils but because there is a sympathetic climate. Speyside is much drier than the west of Scotland, where clouds sweeping in from the Atlantic have their moisture teased from them by the high hills. Strathspey is one of the frostiest regions in Scotland, and pines thrive in a dry cold.

Abernethy may look natural to a casual visitor, yet the hand of man is everywhere revealed. The old Highland term for the Scots pine was 'fir'—it is *fyr* in Denmark. True firs were not part of primeval Caledonia. References to 'fir' abound in documents connected with the Highlands, and in 1693 two men were brought to justice for burning heath in 'Abernethie'. They had incidentally burned much 'fir wood'.

This was a fairly late case of man's misuse of the forests. The cover has been receding since Neolithic times. Trees were burned or felled to provide clearings for agriculture, homes, furniture and firewood. Fires were started to flush out wild beasts, notably the wolf, and wild men—the enemies of those who carried the torches.

Pines were felled and burned for charcoal, which was used in the smelting of iron. For a time, however, the isolation of the Speyside forests were in their favour. It was one thing to fell a tree and quite another to transport it for many miles to a place where the wood might be used. Man then made use of the river and its tributaries. The technological breakthrough came shortly after 1715, when the York Building Company purchased a great deal of valuable Scots pine at Abernethy. It was decided to float the logs down the river, and eventually dams and sluices were installed to control the water levels. Horses drew the trunks to the waterside, where they were customarily peeled and allowed to dry before being floated. At first, rafts of modest size were sent down the main river to Garmouth, but inevitably rafts became larger, more complex, manned by lusty men who held massive oars. About the year 1800 a man could earn over a shilling a day floating timber down the Spey.

When the railway network began to develop, Highland pine,

which was marketed under a number of names, including 'Baltic redwood', was valuable as sleepers for the tracks. Ironically, the entry of steam locomotives into the Spey valley accelerated the forest's decline, each locomotive, chugging to Inverness, being a potential fire-raiser because it emitted sparks as well as smoke. A Mr Selby, visiting Glen More in about 1870, saw "scattered trees, some of which were in a scathed or dying state . . . the solitary and mournful-looking relics of the departed glories of this once well-clad woodland scene". In two world wars further dramatic inroads were made into the pinewoods as lumbermen, some of them from Canada, made their own special contribution to the war effort.

Against this sad chronicle of man's abuse of a bountiful nature can be set details of the efforts made by some landowners to plant, not just reap. Early last century, the sixth Earl of Seafield —son of the man who developed Grantown—added to the family renown by planting over thirty-one million trees. The natural pine woods of the Highlands were already famous in England. Surely the English seed merchants sent their men to Strathspey, as they did to Deeside, to spread sheets around outstanding pines and collect the seeds.

In Abernethy I stood before a patriachal pine which, I was told, is at least 200 years old, but is inappropriately named 'Fairy Tree'. Here was *Pinus sylvestris scotica* in advanced age, still hearty but undoubtedly in decline. Thick roots bulged above the ground before probing the moist acidic earth. Heavy branches swept out almost horizontally, mocking gravity, or soared well above a man's normal range of sight, dwarfing some of the neighbouring pines. The bare ground round about suggested that many people had been here to pay tribute to a worthy giant. An alternative explanation is that in the Highlands the fairies wear hob-nailed boots!

This tree would be a seedling at, say, the period of the earlier Jacobite uprising. Its story would begin in May, with the dispersal of pollen from the male trees—pollen to be absorbed by female flowers set at the end of the annual shoots. On a hot July day—the sort of day when tawny clouds composed of insects waver in the shafts of sunlight—there is a popping in pine woods like Abernethy as the cones burst and seeds are emitted. Then begins the seed's long process of thrusting development—a quest for space and light in which millions of seeds and saplings perish. In due season, the Fairy Tree would rot—and maybe become a nesting place for a pair of crested tits.

In my quest for these fairy-like birds I could have chosen any number of places, some of them more renowned than Abernethy. Crested tits breed up to about the tree line for pines, which approaches 2,000 feet in these parts. For many years the specialist needs of the bird made it a prisoner in the old pine woods, but with vast new conifer forests springing up to maturity in areas in and around Speyside the crested tit is extending its range. It remains a rare bird. The population, estimated at between 300 and 400 pairs, can be much smaller after a really hard winter.

Crested tits are amorous in late April. During the heady courtship days, a male bird offers food to the female, who receives it with head held low and wings shimmering—a sight seen by comparatively few people. Now, in late May, both birds would be food-gathering for their young, if (and there are a number of 'ifs' when seeking crested tits) their nest had not been rifled by a red squirrel. I had already heard of two nests found by a forester. He returned to them a few days later and discovered they had been ravaged.

The best time to watch crested tits is when they have hungry young to feed. At other times, these tiny birds can be infuriatingly evasive. They do not lack confidence, but their feeding and roosting take place among the foliage of a pine, often at a considerable distance from the ground. Try looking upwards for a very small, fairly drab, lively bird at a range of 50 feet!

The first titmouse I saw on leaving the Fairy Tree was a coal tit, another typical bird of the conifer woods. The bird stood on a low branch and allowed me time to take in the main features —shining black head, pale cheeks, white nape patch (seen when it moved).

A view westwards from the road above Tummel Bridge; Schichallion lies on the far left

The oyster-catcher nests beside many Highland rivers

Crested tit perched on the rotten pine stump it has chosen for nesting
in the Speyside forest

A Pictish bull, the cast of an ancient stone carving, in the Highland Folk Museum at Kingussie

A modern Highland beast

I strode along a path that man had beaten out between cushions of blaeberry and ling. The path undulated. When I had lost sight of the Fairy Tree, the main forest track and my car, I was a solitary human figure in the fragrant world of the pines. Now I sought to follow the forester's advice—to look for a rotten pine stump in a small clearing, and I began to walk in steadily-widening circles. This technique is used successfully when seeking cast deer antlers; it ends with the discovery of an antler or the total exhaustion of the walker!

The forest floor undulated and held a tangle of woody growth. Trees muffled sound from the outer world, so that when I stopped I clearly heard a rasping sound as a red squirrel moved up the scaly trunk of a pine. Beholding me over the tip of a low branch, the squirrel chattered and also quivered its tail with annoyance.

A blaeberry-covered knoll lay in an open part of the forest. From near the summit of the knoll protruded the stump of a pine—a stump so rotten it was at the point of collapse. The whole structure moved when I rapped it. I noticed a few twisted twigs plated with grey lichen. Growing near the top of the stump was cranberry and near the roots—lushly green against the light tones of the almost barkless pine—sprouted patches of crowberry and blaeberry, each with fresh green leaves.

A large hole had been driven deep into the stump, from a point about three feet up, and—fortuitously—a flange of old bark gave the hole protection from rain. If, as I hoped, this hole had been made by a crested tit, then it was conceivably a new hole. The species likes to start afresh each spring, the cock titmouse showing eager interest and giving vocal support as the hen works on the task of excavation, removing from the immediate area any tell-tale chips of wood.

I have never seen the nest of crested tit, and on this occasion I could not see to the end of the hole. The eggs are laid in a ball of moss, lined with deer hair, sheep wool or feathers. The crested tit lays a comparatively small clutch, five or six eggs, and incubation lasts for a fortnight.

I rapped the trunk of the rotten pine for a second time and thought I heard a sneeze of irritation from within the hole.

When I had kept watch on the nest of a coal tit, the bird regularly 'sneezed'—but sat tight. Now, as I watched the hole in the Abernethy pine from a distance of a yard, it disgorged the bird I was seeking. A blur of brown sped to a nearby pine and resolved itself into a crested tit.

Here, in real life, was the species that had stared at me from photographs in innumerable books I had read—a rather stocky bird, about the size of a blue tit, brown above, buff underneath. Other features first took the eye—pale cheeks, black bib, crest of black feathers edged with white creating a speckled appearance.

The crested tit scolded me. Its ripple of sound lay somewhere between a thin, metallic trill and a succession of chirps. More rapid trills were to be heard when the bird's mate arrived, stuttering out alarm. I heard all the sounds distinctly though they emanated from the throat of a creature only four and a-half inches long. In the serenity of this old pine wood there was little competing sound.

I stood 10 yards from the nest, but my position was too close for the comfort of this Abernethy pair. I moved further away, standing ankle deep in blaeberry. The birds' outbursts began to subside. I sat on a patch of springy vegetation, and the crested tits began a shuttle service with food. When a bird alighted daintily on a lichen-covered twig it stood for a few seconds, the brown upperparts harmonizing with the tones of the dead stump. Then the tit flew to the nesting hole, briefly depressing its crest as it entered. The bird reappeared moments later, leaving the entrance with swift and purposeful flight.

The red squirrel scolded me as I returned to the Fairy Tree. I felt like scolding the squirrel, a nest-robber. When a squirrel approaches a crested tit nest there is nothing the diminutive birds can do to protect it; they simply fly around, calling loudly, and their very distress will confirm in the squirrel's mind that there are eggs or young birds to be taken.

Away from the nest, young birds perch with shivering wings, begging for food. Summer is spent mainly on the crown of the Abernethy pine. There could be a time in winter—a hard winter, sparse in food—when the crested tits might benefit from the activities of squirrels, visiting ransacked pine cones and extracting from them the odd seeds the squirrels left behind.

There was, in Abernethy, that deep hush found in old churches. Few birds moved. A tawny owl watched me gravely from its daytime roost. I understand that the long-eared owl has been observed in Abernethy. Half a mile behind me, the crested tits would be continuing their shuttle service with food, as their ancestors have done in Abernethy for many thousands of years.

5

COCK OF THE WOODS

At every corner of the forester's road near Boat of Garten I stared quickly ahead, hoping to see a cock capercaillie isolated from its forest haunts because it was standing on the light grey track. Theoretically, a caper is hard to miss. The length of the splendid cock bird is 35 inches, or almost a yard. A forester at Nethy Bridge told me to look for something "as big as a littlish turkey"! The female is lighter in colour and only about half the cock's weight.

Once, when I had stopped the car, there was a noisy whirr of wings. A hen caper rose from the edge of the track. When its forward drive had enough power, the bird developed a short glide, during which its wings were downcurved. I saw a rufous breast as the caper turned to sweep majestically between pines a hundred yards away. For its size, the bird was nimble, sure, accurate.

With memories of the crested tits still fresh in the mind, I chuckled at the thought of giant caper and midget titmouse living in the same pine forest habitat where their specialist natures have imprisoned them.

Pliny gave the first recorded description of a capercaillie. No bird except the ostrich grew to be so heavy. "Because it is so fat, it sits motionless on the ground practically the whole time and is easily caught by the hunter. . . . It loses its taste in aviaries. It kills itself in old age by holding its breath." This entertaining hotch-potch of fact and fancy is understandable

with reference to such a large, bizarre bird. The forester at
Nethy Bridge who told me about caper in Abernethy spoke as
though expecting me to be incredulous that the bird gobbles
down grit to assist it in the initial breakdown of its food. Nearly
everything that is known about the capercaillie is fascinating,
sometimes grotesque.

The pine forest offers a caper much more than pine needles. I
arrived at a time when the ground vegetation had greened-up
with the coming of spring. There were young shoots to be eaten,
and the leaves of the blaeberry would be appetising. In summer
the caper would so gorge itself on berries its droppings would
have a purple hue. The forester had watched capercaillie leaving
the forestland to gorge themselves on the grain from stooked corn.

Capercaillie! The name is as strange as the bird. It should be
pronounced 'capp-er-kailyee' and comes from a Gaelic name,
capull coille. The alternative spelling is capercailzie, which to
me looks and sounds awkward, while having a North Country
flavour. My forest friend and his colleagues spoke of 'caper'. The
name is said to be derived from 'horse of the woods'—from a
similarity between the cock bird's spring serenade and the clip-
clop of a horse's hooves. I found a medieval reference, connected
with the north-east of England, to 'wode-henne'. I prefer the
frequently-used name 'cock of the woods', for there is a jaunti-
ness about it.

My encounter with a cock caper was momentary. I had
motored to a T-junction, from which I looked across broken
ground to a number of flat-topped trees. A forester called them
"caper trees", but the pine has not necessarily been trampled
flat by roosting caper. The topmost branches of a Scots pine tend
to spread out when the trees have lost their leading shoots. It
is always possible that a caper—or the closely-related black
grouse—was responsible for the missing shoots!

I saw the caper rise with a few powerful wing beats to enter
the umbrella-like foliage of a group of pines without sound or
subsequent trace. Sometimes a caper might be seen silhouetted
against a grey sky on the very top of a pine, looking like a
majestic weather vane.

In poor light, a cock caper looks black. Given reasonably bright conditions, a variety of tones can be seen: dark grey on the neck, dark green on the breast, dark brown on the back. There is brown on the wings, which also have grey and white markings. The belly of the bird is flecked with white. The head is set off by scarlet wattles. The bill, thick and greyish, is "hooked like an eagle's beak", in the picturesque language of the forester.

G. B. Kearey photographed the cock capercaillie in Abernethy in 1938. For years this photograph was the only one in existence of a free-ranging bird in Britain. Now a host of colour photographs permit us to study the bird's form and coloration at leisure. Photographs fix a pose and reveal details of plumage in a way that is difficult to recall from seeing birds briefly in the wild. Colour films are even more informative.

The mating season begins in late March or early April. To see the display of the cock capers, it is necessary to get out of bed before dawn. Arrive in the misty, dripping woods as the robin begins to sing. The robin appears to be the pinewood equivalent of the skylark and is known in some areas of the Continent as 'the capercaillie clock'. Devoted caper-watchers are in position at about 3-30 am, and if they know their ground well they position themselves where they can overlook the area —usually a glade—favoured by the big grouse. Here cock birds come together, work themselves into a passion, make grotesque movements and utter strange sounds.

When displaying, a cock caper is like a contortionist. It stands with drooping wings. The uplifted tail is also spread out, the dark feathers forming an almost perfect semi-circle. The bird upstretches its neck, throws its head well back, distends its throat and incidentally reveals its feathery 'beard'. The fairly docile bird of a few minutes before becomes fearsome, inflated. It is an interesting rather than a pretty sight.

The caper struts, jumps and flaps its wings. Even more grotesque than the prancing and the displaying is the bird's serenade—a series of sounds which may be uttered before the displaying actually begins. There are clicking noises—tchik-

tchek. The sounds follow each other in quickening succession, climaxed by what resembles the noise of a cork suddenly popping from a wine bottle, followed by a burping, or a strange bagpipish wheeze.

Rival cocks are threatened, sometimes fought, rarely injured or killed. The females can be in a receptive mood, croaking responsively and flying down to be mated, or not impressed. Said the forester: "Sometimes they seem bored; they just fly off!" To his knowledge, no-one had been attacked in Abernethy by a cock capercaillie suffering from spring fever, but there are parts of Scotland where attacks on man have occurred. The capercaillie is doubtless bold in its ways because there is little in a pinewood to offer it serious competition—except man.

Human predacity on the capercaillie began in the earliest times. Bones of the birds ended up in the kitchen middens of Early Man. Caper were to be found in many parts of Britain during the heyday of the pine forest, but as the forests declined so did the caper stocks. When the Atlantic phase of weather developed, both pines and caper fared badly. They had thrived in the dry cold of former years, just as the caper of today prefer the relatively dry eastern part of Scotland to the damper, mistier west.

There were fears in Scotland as early as the seventeenth century that the caper would be wiped out. The Scottish Parliament enacted that "caperkayllies" should not be bought or sold. Yet the stock became extinct in the 1780s. The last two native birds were possibly those shot on Deeside in 1785. Less than fifty years later—as already related—the caper had returned to the Highlands. Swedish birds were shipped in and released on the estates of Lord Breadalbane. Meanwhile, in 1831, a Game Act had been drawn up. No mention of the capercaillie was made in it because at that time the capercaillie was extinct in Britain.

How the capercaillie reached the Speyside haunts which now suit it so well is not known for certain, beyond a story related by H. A. Gilbert and Arthur Brook. They stayed with a Speyside man who claimed to have brought caper into the district, collecting eggs in Perthshire, transporting them over the Drumochter Pass, and putting them into the nests of greyhens— the females of the black grouse.

Before travelling to Scotland I had an interesting apprentice-ship to capercaillie in the English Lake District. Bill Grant, the forester-in-charge of Grizedale, on the Furness Fells, collected caper eggs from his native Aberdeenshire and released the birds that hatched into a pinewood area. Bill reintroduced the capercaillie into England after a lapse of over 200 years.

The experiment began in the spring of 1968, when Bill Grant obtained three clutches of eggs from gamekeepers and foresters in north-east Scotland. Placed in boxes containing hay and hot water bottles, the eggs were driven 300 miles back to Grizedale. Two hatched, but the chicks died.

In the following spring, 12 eggs were obtained, and 10 of them hatched out during the return journey, Bill Grant having taken broody bantams with him. He kept some of the chicks warm by dropping them inside his shirt! At Grizedale, nine chicks were reared, being fed mainly on turkey crumbs and maggots. The birds were apparently kept for too long and died, mainly through injuries received as they dashed themselves against the wire of the pen. This problem crops up repeatedly with captive caper-caillie. A Speyside forester said the tendency was offset when birch was placed against the wire, cushioning the shock of impact.

In 1970, Bill Grant heard that a tract of pinewood was to be clear-felled. Many caper nests were likely to be destroyed. He arranged for the threatened nests to be marked and once again took the road to the Highlands. The nests lay in deep heather, well away from the road. Eggs were transported back to the car in cardboard boxes which had been partly filled with sheep wool plucked from the fences on the outward walk. The eggs were then placed under bantams. Almost all of them hatched out at Grizedale. Forty chicks—25 cocks, 15 hens—were released into the pinewoods at the end of August.

Here, in mid-April during the following year, I made a dawn

Front view of a displaying capercaillie cock being reared in captivity

Speyside—viewed north-eastwards from the lower slopes of Cairn Gorm, looking over Loch Morlich and Glenmore Forest

patrol hoping to hear the weird arias of cock birds. Maybe the stock was too young, or the centre of occupation had shifted to another part of the forest. As dawn came to the comparatively young pine woods a robin was heard singing. A few other small birds contributed to the dawn chorus, which is impoverished in thickly-conifered areas. In the evening—a chilling grey evening—I watched a young caper hen feeding on a pine. Balanced on a slender branch, the bird plucked and swallowed clusters of needles. Seen distantly, the capercaillie looked drab, but when I had sneaked closer and focussed binoculars I saw an exciting medley of tones. There was the russet breast, and much white on the sides of the body.

The pine tree was clearly being visited regularly. Some of the branches were half-stripped of needles. Deftly the six-pound bird walked along the branch, which it grasped with strong claws showing below the well-feathered legs. The branch swayed gently. Pine needles were being wrenched off by a strong grey beak, and as the bird ate it was possible to see beard-like feathers at the neck. Pine needles fill the crop, sustain the bird's life in hard times, but do little else. It has been discovered through experiments in Scotland that a capercaillie on this fixed diet loses weight in the midst of winter.

The forester I met in Abernethy did far more than tell me about capercaillie. He took me to a nest. Finding a sitting caper is a matter of chance in a forest extending over thousands of acres. One year he found five nests, and in the following year— when he looked even more intensely—he could not locate one. Once he decided to take a photograph, turned from a nest and walked away sufficiently far to bring into play his tele-photo lens. Raising his camera, he had difficulty in finding the nest through the viewer, yet he knew to within a few feet where the hen bird was crouching!

The nest I visited was untypical of the breed. A hen usually selects a site close up to a tree, invariably a pine. Many are to be found in thick heather. Our bird was in an area where timber clearance had taken place; there was a big glade, littered with the remnants of larches, each of them tasselled with hard grey

E

lichen. The nearest standing timber, some young spruce, was about forty yards away.

We approached the nest between cushions of blaeberry and heaps of rotten branches. A few larch trees lay around, one of them not totally disconnected from its roots, so that the branches were greening up with the spring. The forester had tied some dead grass round a branch as an indicator. We stood near it and he invited me to find the nest. It was about ten yards away.

I made the mistake of looking for the form of the capercaillie when I should have sought a patch of varied colours—a reddish-brown blotch partly tucked away under a latticework of dead branches. When a hen caper returns to a nest, one marvels that such an enormous bird will be able to remain undetected. The caper shuffles lower and lower, covering the eggs closely. When undisturbed, the bird holds up its head and looks around, but a suspicious bird lowers its head and crouches even lower.

The nest was pointed out to me at a range of five feet. I saw a sparkle in the sitting bird's eye. There was the stolid form of the hooked beak, which was lead-grey in colour, and the finery of plumage: rufous, mottled with black and grey. The forester told me the bird was covering five eggs.

After slowly walking around the nest, I approached it even closer, deciding that if the bird remained I would photograph it and retreat immediately. If the bird flew off, I would photograph the nest and hasten away. The capercaillie did not move. I edged forward until the viewer of the camera was filled with the glory of the plumage. I saw my own reflection in the bird's bright eye. The caper had stiffened; its muscles must have been as taut as watchsprings.

We stared at each other, then I strode away.

A hundred yards distant lay a litter of shells where a pheasant had hatched out a brood and taken the young birds away. A meadow pipit left its nest when I was about to accidentally tread on it. I saw that the nest was enfolded by coarse grasses. Peering into it, I saw the bright gapes of young birds.

On higher, marginal land, where the pines begin to peter out, spring is enlivened by the black grouse. The cocks gather at old tourney grounds, the *leks*, and indulge in a ritual dance, prancing with drooped wings and tails raised to reveal the frilly white of feathers. In recline, the tail of a blackcock is lyre-shaped —the traditional adornment to the bonnets of Scottish regiments.

Blackcocks do not break the stillness of dawn fiercely, nor quaintly like the capercaillie, but with a pigeon-like *roocooing*. It has a lulling effect. I have heard birds calling in the late afternoon and have found the display grounds, where coarse vegetation is padded down until, by the end of the season, it resembles coconut matting. The hen birds are smaller than the cocks and are called greyhens; in fact, they have a brown hue.

The forester seemed to detest the black grouse more than the capercaillie. He told me of a caper drive in Abernethy during the previous January when over a dozen birds were slain, but added: "We're not out to exterminate them. The trouble is that the caper is too successful. You find it all over the place. It damages trees, but we can tolerate a certain amount of damage, and, after all, the caper was using the woods long before man came along and took over."

A commendable sentiment.

6

FICKLE SPEY

In April, the snow begins to melt on the High Cairngorms—
and you can smell the thaw! To detect this 'snow bree', go out
and about on a warm and windy day after a dry spell. Walk to
the places where the burns emerge from the hillsides. Sniff the
air. You will also smell spring.

Snow water is obviously very cold. Each burn contributes its
quota to the tributary streams, which surge into the Spey
having been stained pale-brown by peat. When fish feel snow
water coursing around them they tend to become sluggish,
unresponsive to the angler's bait. The angler, in turn, tries to
avoid wading in the river where his legs would soon be
refrigerated.

The snow does not melt and run off the Cairngorms in a short,
violent spate. Some of the streams tumbling down the hills all
summer are being fed almost entirely by the snowfields. I have
been told of patches of everlasting snow. If the winter is mild,
the snow melts earlier than usual, and sometimes a quick thaw
is attended by heavy rain. The Spey comes out in furious spate
—and it is reputedly the swiftest river in Scotland.

The Spey tumbles swiftly off the hills beyond Laggan, flows at
a moderate rate through the wetlands and Loch Insh, becomes
lively again to Grantown and then descends about 800 feet
between here and the sea, where it has developed so much force
its darker waters can be seen clearly against the turbulent competition of the flow tides of Moray Firth.

People have spoken of "the fickle Spey". Many people have drowned in its waters. The weather at Grantown might be dry, but storm clouds mass around the high hills or there is an isolated thunderclap and storm in the upper strath. Suddenly, unexpectedly, the voice of the Spey at Grantown becomes deeper. The river rises several feet in a few hours.

I contemplated the Spey from the parapet of the bridge near Grantown. A sandpiper trilled. A departing dipper gave a metallic zit, zit. The river was low and so its voice was high— a tinkling voice of water surging against exposed rocks and shingle. Little snow had fallen on the Cairngorms during the winter and therefore little melt-water had arrived. The spring weather was, as usual, rather dry.

Look at Strathspey from the heights, and you can pick out the course of the river not only from the sight of gleaming water but from the lines of trees mustered on its banks. The ancestors of the salmon and sea trout which move up the river would pass between banks that were even more thickly forested with birch and pine. The pattern of the spawning runs was set not long after the great ice sheet had disappeared—and it endures, though on a much smaller scale.

Early Man hunted and fished. Doubless he speared or netted the salmon and sea trout. Medieval visitors to Strathspey marvelled at the abundance of salmon, and even as late as the 1850s the Duke of Richmond's waters could yield an average of 57,000 salmon and grilse every year. That same century saw a decline in the salmon stocks for various reasons, one being a measure of pollution from the whisky distilleries and another the wholesale netting of salmon around the river mouth.

The anglers who gather in the hotels and boarding houses in anticipation of a run of salmon today do so for enjoyment, prestige and possibly a little glory. The Gaelic names for the fish have almost been forgotten. There was *bradan* for salmon, *breac* for trout, *geadas* for pike, and *tarragan* for the char found in and on either side of Loch Insh. A local man told me of the latest state of the river, and said the anglers had to be content with sea trout, or enjoy their fishing retrospectively through

incessant taproom talk. In the Spey, a seeker after salmon tends
to use well-seasoned flies like Greenwell's Glory and Peter Ross.

From what I had seen of the Spey I could not picture it as
a river in which salmon did much leaping. I half-closed my eyes
and daydreamed of the salmon of my recollection—of fish
springing from deep pools, bodies arching into crescent shapes
which suddenly straighten out as the fish seek the maximum
amount of lift. A desperate salmon can leap over six feet—and
does in some northern parts of Scotland. In the Spey, the depth
of water is vital. A salmon held captive by low water in a pool
near Grantown might be able to move if the river rose a trifling
two inches.

Mr Hamish Marshall, of Grantown, told me that the local
quest for salmon begins on 11th February. Only the most
optimistic—or innocent—of anglers would expect to see salmon
moving then. The main run occurs during the latter part of
March. All depends on the river level, and during the springtime
when I visited Strathspey there was a drought.

The water level is but one of several hazards faced by salmon.
Near the river mouth are nets and seals. Some salmon taken
from the river bear the marks left by the suckers of lampreys. If
there is a good run, salmon get to the Grantown reaches by May
and go on into the Truim, over 80 miles from the sea, during
the first week in June. A keeper caught a fresh-run salmon in the
Truim on 28th March, 1971, the earliest date known.

Old men at Grantown were shaking their heads because hardly
any salmon were moving. It had been the same during the
previous year. I heard of the "good old days" and what were
referred to as Norwegian fish—salmon that were blueish in
colour and present in the Spey from September onwards. Now
there's just an odd 'blue' among the commoner pinkish salmon.

Men who are wise to the river stare at the water and then
locate the form of a salmon—which may be scarcely moving
against the peat-stained flow. Taking a second glance, the wise
men will tell you how long it has been in fresh water. They
cannot prove their statement, of course, and they could conceivably be wrong, but experience over many years leads them

to guess fairly accurately. The colour of the sojourning salmon darkens. Some fish go almost black.

From February until the end of May, anglers operating in the Grantown area go hopefully to the river with their brown and golds and Toby spoons, spinning for salmon. Early in the season, anglers use the largest flies they can find. Some notable beats have names with local renown—Tulcan, Cromdale, Knockando —but not everyone can fish in the most prolific reaches. About Grantown, a man can fish for a season—except on Sundays—for a modest £5, as compared with the £250 or so a week demanded at the reaches lying nearer the sea.

Fishing on what is, for the Highlands, a shoestring is possible because of the Strathspey Angling Improvement Association, which is based on Grantown. It was formed in 1914, renting a stretch of the Spey from the Seafield Estate for 10s a year. This concession arose through the generosity of the then Countess of Seafield. She was deliriously happy when, after a long law suit, the whisky distillers had been instructed to keep their burnt ale —by-product of the main process—out of the river.

I discovered that angling elsewhere can be expensive. It is usual for a syndicate of, say, five anglers, to pay the fees. One man paid out over £70 for a week's sport. He was fortunate, and more than paid for his holiday through selling the salmon he caught.

The average weight of a Spey salmon is 10 pounds, but everyone likes to hear about the monster fish taken from the river. The rod and line season closes on 31st October, but some fish are taken for spawning in artificial conditions. One such, a cock salmon landed at Craigellachie in November, weighed 34 pounds and was possibly two pounds heavier at its first appearance in the mouth of the Spey in spring. A hen salmon taken from the Spey so that its eggs could be coaxed from it weighed 19 pounds and was found to contain 6 pounds of roe. Indeed, a 12-pounder salmon might carry about 9,000 eggs.

It amazes me that any salmon survive to spawn in the head-reaches of the Spey and its tributaries. Some of the angling methods of the past were wasteful in the extreme. Salmon run up the river Dulnain, which flows through Carrbridge, and here a 'gentleman' of years ago thought nothing of killing 160 salmon in a night. The most ingenious fisherman was possibly the householder near "the passage boat of Gartenmore", who—according to Shaw, in his *History of Moray*—cast a salmon net into a pool below the wall of the house each night. "A small rope, tied to the net and brought in at the window, had a bell hung at it, which rung when a salmon came into and shook the net."

Salmon running up the Spey not only travel far—they reach high and remote places, the most thrustful entering lochs in the High Cairngorms. Mr Hamish Marshall has regularly found them in burns at 1,000 feet above sea level. One fish that was ripe unto spawning lay in a burn only two feet wide.

The gravelly areas where the eggs are deposited (*redds*) are the places where hen fish acquire mates. The cock salmon has formed a hooked snout for the season. It is a useful adornment for dealing with rivals, not—as some people suppose—a convenient implement for excavating the redds. The spawned hen fish (*kelt*) makes its way back to the sea. Most kelts perish; they do not undertake a second spawning run. Kelts tend to respond readily to an angler's spoons and minnows. If these fish have proceeded far down river they may have 'got a belly on'. An inexperienced angler, hooking a kelt, bears it home triumphantly as a prize catch!

I mentioned to a seasoned Spey angler my amazement that a salmon is reputed not to feed while in the river. He quietly pointed out that if a fish continued to eat while on the spawning run it would soon dispose of the available stocks of food—and maybe young fish of its own kind. "I wouldn't like to have the job of feeding a salmon. There's no other river fish to match it in size, except the largest of the pike."

Colonel Thornton was an obsessive angler. His fingers twitched whenever he saw a river. On a July day about 1796 he "took the nets, intending to draw the river and Loch Insh, which we conceived full of fish". Another time, he went to Aviemore for dinner at 8 pm, "having sent a servant on before with a fine pike, which we found ready to dress". Loch Insh remains a lurking place for fine pike, its water being moderately deep; the loch has a muddy bed. Hamish Marshall has seen a 18½ pound pike taken from it—and that did not break any records.

The innkeeper at Aviemore told Colonel Thornton about some prodigious pike in the Spey. One pike was a nuisance; the innkeeper had hooked it on three successive days, but each time the tackle broke and the hooks were lost. The enraged innkeeper shot at the pike four times without effect!

Colonel Thornton rode to the riverside and sent the horses back to Aviemore. Alas, his fishing-hook was in the saddlebag of one of them, but local people told him that if he threw in a living animal—any living animal, even a dog—the pike would instantly respond.

"I adjusted a strong trimmer-hook with a very moderate swivel; and, accordingly, threw in a live bait; the instant the rapid stream carried it down a pike came at me with infinite eagerness, making the whole water foam, and ran me across the stream and into his hold, about forty feet." The innkeeper was ecstatic at the thought of recovering his many lost hooks. "I gave the pike some time to gorge, and then began to play him, having excellent sport for ten minutes. The landlord prepared himself with the landing net, but before it was time to use it he [the fish!] broke his hold."

The Colonel sent a man to Aviemore for the hook. He added fresh bait and cast again. The pike responded instantly, and he gave the fish time to eat the bait. The Colonel believed strongly in patience, recommending that an angler "read a sermon between the times of striking at his fish and his striking at the bait; and, in the failure of a sermon, possibly a chapter in the *Pilgrim's Progress* might be found a pretty substitute." Despite his patience, the Colonel failed again.

Now he "threw in my bait (a very tempting silver-coloured trout) with a pair of snap-hooks that had never failed me. Back came the pike, and this time it had a real battle on its hands". The fish was landed, being pronounced "most noble", but the

Colonel was reticent about giving a specific weight for the fish. Was the pike far less impressive than the story he told about it?

The most curious type of 'fishing' in the Spey concern fresh-water mussels, locally called oysters. They lie in the rocky bed, and some of them contain pearls. Amateurs, seeking them with more enthusiasm than knowledge, enter the river and feel for the mussels with their toes. Their enthusiasm evaporates if they do not find pearls within a reasonable time.

The professional goes doggedly on, for comparatively small returns, but with the Micawber-like hope of better days. Boats, even coracles, were once employed, and the river's glare was overcome when boxes with glass bottoms were made and pushed just below the surface for viewing the river bed.

The char of Loch Insh are novel. Small communities of char inhabit various lochs, usually deep lochs, a case in point being Loch Einich, in the far Cairngorms. The once-migratory char became land-locked in various parts of Britain after the Ice Ages. Though the old migratory urge was almost lost, char at Loch Insh do have greater scope for movement. The average weight of these 'Arctic char', said Mr Marshall, is about 1½ pounds.

7

BEEF FROM BADENOCH

For over an hour I contemplated a herd of Highland cattle. The impulse to do no more than stop, stare and motor on came from the weather, which had been fretful all morning, drawing a grey curtain across the Cairngorms. In the rapidly-worsening light, colour drained from objects near at hand. The road I was taking —from Nethy bridge to Coylumbridge—became wet, reflective, faintly silvered by mist-filtered light. The rain that followed was not fierce and directional, pattering on the car roof, but a drizzling rain, the proverbial Scotch mist.

To the right of the road was land only a shade better than moorland, dotted by Scots pines. To the left lay a pasture of generous size on which shaggy Highland cattle were tugging at the spring green herbage. Other beasts, lying down, stared vacantly into space from beneath frills of coarse hair, and their jaws moved rhythmically as they chewed the cud. Few trees sprouted from the enclosed land on which the cattle were grouped. On a near skyline—murky in the mist—were some of the outriders of Glen More, the Queen's Forest.

Economics apart, the Highlander is among the most attractive of our native cattle. Other motorists thought so. After I had parked my car 100 yards from the nearest beast, I regularly heard the squeal of brakes as other vehicles stopped briefly, their occupants chattering and pointing and clicking cameras. The cattle ignored us totally, obsessed with a prolonged quest for fresh protein after an austere winter

Inevitably, I was reminded of paintings of the Highlands made by Victorian visitors. The artists of a century ago were fascinated by the native cattle, which they tended to use like pieces of stage scenery. They posed Highland cattle on wine-red moors that were a-swirl with mist, the vapours adding to a sense of desolation. Or they stood the beasts with their forefeet in the water of lochans—sometimes, no doubt, as an attempt by the artist to cover up his inadequacies in coping with bovine legs!

I was able to take my contemplation of the cattle beyond the romantic stage. I had a check list of good points about the Highlanders. The helpful secretary of the Highland Cattle Society had sent me a copy of the preface to the first Herd Book, prepared in 1885, in which the main characteristics were listed. The prose was fine, tinged with love, as befits animals that "have long been considered as the handsomest of our cattle . . . often selected to adorn the parks of southern noblemen".

The compilers of the preface gave most space to consideration of the head, to which the Highland beast "owes his great favour among artists". The bull nearest to my car seemed to measure up well to the requirements. It was broad between the eyes and short from eyes to the point of the muzzle. Frankly, I could not see the ideally "bright and full" eyes for hair!

The horns were clear for all to see; they gave the animal a very fierce look that belied its manner. Not once during my vigil near the herd did I see a beast use its horns pugnaciously. The best type of Highland bull (and this was one of them) has strong horns; they "come level out of the head, slightly inclining forwards and also slightly rising towards the points". Two opinions were stated to prevail about a cow's horns. Generally, they come more squarely out of the head than in the male; they rise sooner, and are somewhat longer. The other taste is for a back set curve and very wide sweep.

Argue about this as you might, the horns of a Highlander must be well-set, giving "the animal a stamp of nobility which causes it to attract the attention of any stranger who might pass heedlessly by animals of other breeds as merely cows, bulls, or oxen". When the tenth car was braked, and the tenth excited group of people stared at the cattle, I could see what was meant.

I skipped the section of the preface dealing with the neck and shoulder. In connection with the body, there was the usual cattleman's point about a good straight back—"any slight sinking or hollow is most decidedly objectionable". It is virtuous for the ribs to spring boldly out, being well-rounded and deep. A Highland beast should be "set wide between the forelegs, and it should move with great dignity and style, as this is considered to be one of the most reliable evidences of careful and true breeding".

Wavy-brown hair thatched the podgy, low-set bodies of the Highlanders I saw. Ideally, there should be a great profusion of hair that is long, gracefully waved, "very much as in what dog-breeders denote wavy-coated retrievers". Abundant hair, and a good thickness of skin, are the natural outcome of animals exposed to a severe northern weather without being molly-coddled.

Experts speculate at length about the origins of our native cattle. Sometimes they do not pay enough regard to the rapid changes in appearance that are possible in a fairly short time when one or two men have some new ideas about what is needed. Yet the Highland beast looks to be of ancient type. The preface to the Herd Book stated: "Some have maintained that there never was an aboriginal breed, while others have maintained that there was such a breed, and that it is now represented by the wild cattle of Chillingham Park." It was the first time I had heard of such a comparison, and I did not dwell on it.

More certain is a reference to two types or 'classes'. The compilers of the Herd Book specified the West Highland, which was sometimes called the kyloe—a generally dark beast found in its purest form in the Western Islands—and the mainland beast, which was rather larger in size because of better pasturage, "not uniformly of a black colour" and common to the mainland of northern Scotland and the county of Argyle. The cattle near Coylumbridge were only the second herd of this breed I had seen,

there having been another fine group to the north of the Sma'
Glen.

Films about the Highlands feature flocks of sheep, mainly of
the black-faced breed, and a few hundred books have related what
happened when Highland families were cleared off their traditional lands to make way for more flocks. Yet long before sheep
spread in bleating hordes across the Highlands, cattle were a
vital part of the economy, and they outnumbered sheep. The
cattle were wintered at the main settlements in glen and strath,
but in spring—when the high hills greened up again—they were
driven to the sheilings, temporary settlements on hilly land.

Tending the summering cattle was a job mainly for women
and boys. Their shelters were buildings made of stone, thatched
with heather or rush, warmed by turf fires, on which cooking
also took place, and having beds composed of straw.

Such a migration gave the home acres a change, if not a rest.
The cattle could take advantage of the flush of new grass—and
were also partly responsible for the deforestation of the hills.
Grazing on the heights, the cattle had fresh breezes on their
faces and could escape from the marshy places, thus avoiding
the worst of the summer fly menace. The goodness of milk which
people drew from the cows was locked up in the form of cheese
or butter.

Picture, then, people and cattle following old trods to the
hills. The pastoral people of Aviemore and Kincraig went to the
upper valley of the Dulnain, and those of Rothiemurchus sought
land around Loch Einich. Laggan people turned to the land
around the source of the Spey. They responded to an impulse
affecting hill folk in many parts of the world, but those days
are long gone and difficult to recall.

The word 'shieling' appears on the maps of remote places, but
on the ground there remains just a scattering of stones to mark
the old shelters, and we can only dimly imagine what shieling
life was like. Some of the old songs have survived to give us
something of its lyrical quality. They are simple, rather sad little
pieces, best rendered in the original Gaelic. This is an anglicized
example: "But 'tis pity that I and my sweetheart of flowing

locks were not in the little green clump, where the wood-pigeon will crow; the rushy thicket in which would be the roebuck—and the heather around is in dark green folds".

It was possible late in the eighteenth century to sample sheiling life. Colonel Thornton visited a "boothée" or "sheelin", which he described as a cottage made of turf, "the dairy-house where the Highland shepherds, or grasiers, live with their herds and flocks and, during the fine season, make butter and cheese, gather juniper berries which, in parts of the Highlands abound, and sell for a good price". The Colonel noticed that "their whole furniture consists of a few horn spoons, their milking utensils, a couch formed of sods to lie on, and a rug to cover them. Their food, oat-cakes, butter or cheese, and often the coagulated blood of their cattle spread on their bannocks; their drink, milk, whey, and sometimes, by way of indulgence, whisky".

Entering a *boothée* on a rainy day, Colonel Thornton watched an old lady adding some faggots of dry juniper to the fire. "We got ourselves as dry and comfortable as our lodging and hostess . . . could make us. My landlady might be on the wrong side of forty-five, much wizened and dried by the smoke, but had a cheerful countenance and, as is usual with most ladies, a prodigious desire of conversing, which was [because of language difficulties] totally denied us."

When summer waned, people and cattle returned to the townships. Surplus beasts would be sold at old marketing centres like Pitmain, at the edge of Kingussie. Such pastoral communities were based largely on personal honesty, for many of the laws were accepted but unwritten. Theft was naturally abhorred, and three men who stole cattle and sheep at 'Bellintome' (near Grantown) in 1697 were made to linger in the dungeon of Castle Grant and were then hanged. Another offender had an ear severed, was scourged—and banished.

In cases of theft, it was necessary for charges to be pressed against the guilty people. A man called Mungo became a laughing stock because when his fine white ox was stolen he made only feeble attempts to recover it—and did not succeed. The incident occurred towards the end of the eighteenth century and

was recorded by Mrs Grant of Laggan. Mungo took his servant
with him on a journey to "the shealing of Drymen [Drummin]",
at the foot of the "Corryarick", where he was credibly informed
his white favourite might be found. He saw the conspicuous
beast quietly grazing, unguarded and alone; but having thought
better of the matter, or supposing the creature looked very happy
where he was, he quietly returned without him.

"Being as deficient in true Highland caution as in courage,
he very innocently told, when he came home, that he had seen
his ox and left it there. The disgrace attending this failure was
beyond the power of a lowland heart to conceive. He was, in
all his life after, called Mungo of the White Ox; and to this day
it is accounted very ill-bred to mention an ox of that colour
before any of his descendants."

Not all the stock cattle reared on the hills remained in the
locality. There was an export trade of Highland cattle in the
Middle Ages. Gradually there evolved a pattern of seasonal
cattle movements to England that reached staggering proportions. England was not always welcoming towards Scottish
cattle, its graziers fearing a decline in the profitability of their
own stock. For a brief period in the seventeenth century, Highland cattle were discriminated against and efforts were made to
breed more cattle in England.

Yet the demand for meat was insatiable. English towns were
growing quickly through industrialization, and the demand for
more meat was met readily by cattle bred at the periphery of
Britain—in Scotland, Ireland and Wales—and driven into
England to be fattened off and slaughtered. The hills grew the
beef, and tough men faced an austere countryside, vicious
weather and rogues of all kinds to deliver it on the hoof to the
marketing centres. Some of the Scottish cattle carried with them
more than the flavour of the Highlands. Sir Walter Scott noted
that the hair at the tail end was knotted as a protection for the
beasts from the spells of witches.

In early autumn, the Highlands seemed to erupt black cattle.
The droves moved like turgid streams along the old tracks. Many
Island cattle were driven across the Corrieyairack Pass to join

Greenshank, photographed on migration, a species less common on Speyside than it was

The Cairngorm plateau from Beinn a Bhuird

up with the Great North Road at about Dalwhinnie. Another route lay through Lochaber, Badenoch, Rannoch and Atholl, then proceeding through the Sma' Glen to the tryst at Crieff. Beasts reared in Ross-shire passed through the main valley of the Spey. Each main stream had its tributaries, and John Tindall, referring to the period around 1810, mentioned that "many thousands of these [kyloes] are annually exiled from their favourite haunts, the Grampian Hills, pass through Yorkshire and other counties in large herds and, if not purchased before, end their toilsome journey in the vicinity of the metropolis, indulged once more with a respite from fatigue, grow fat in smiling pastures, and finally find their way to Smithfield".

What had troubled me, when considering the subject of Highland beef, was an apparent discrepancy between the noble Highland cattle I saw in Speyside—those beasts with the long, wavy-brown hair—and references in the records of the droving trade to "black cattle". The solution came with an inquiry to the Highland Cattle Society. Black cattle were once very numerous and, indeed, there are still many in Scotland. They are of a similar breed to those of the best-known colour, and there is no difference as regards registration in the Herd Book.

While pondering on the droving trade I had therefore to consider mainly the 'kyloe', that West Highland type. The custom of swimming the beasts from their Island nurseries across the kyles to the mainland, provides one explanation of the name. It has also been suggested that the word is merely a corruption of the Gaelic word signifying 'Highland'.

Stated the authors of the preface to the first Herd Book: "The normal colour of the Kyloe was black, and in the recollection of some who are still alive no other colour was known in the leading folds of the West. The pure Kyloe seems also to have been smaller and shaggier than the Highlander, but whether this was a distinctive feature of this class of the breed, or whether it arose from the cattle being kept in a purer state and more exposed to the elements than the mainland cattle, it is not easy to say. It is only within comparatively recent years that the

F

colours which are now so much in favour with breeders became common among the West Highland cattle, and the first animals of colour seem to have been introduced from Perthshire."

Sir Walter Scott knew all about droving, being descended from a drover. He wrote: "The cattle which were the staple commodity of the mountains were escorted down to fairs, on the borders of the Lowlands, by a party of Highlanders, with their arms rattling about them". Drovers were allowed to carry arms at a time when this was generally banned following the Jacobite rebellion. The Highlanders "dealt in all honour and good faith with their Southern customers. A fray indeed would sometimes arise, when the Lowlandmen, chiefly Borderers, who had to supply the English market, opposed their cudgels to the naked broadswords."

The drovers, like the denizens of the shielings, had their lilting Gaelic songs. A translation into English of one of them concerns Badenoch and declares: "What stout fellows the drovers were when they got on the move. The Badenoch men with herds from the moors to the sea's edge, and Clark, a gentleman at their head. MacFarlane was there and MacMillan, and Macintyre from Ruthven; if they stand firm for their price, the King himself is no better off than the farmer." Cattle were marketed in Speyside early last century; it suited drovers who were passing through Badenoch. Such a sale was known as a tryst, and Mrs Grant of Rothiemurchus, writing in 1914, mentioned its existence at Pitmain, near Kingussie. Cattle purchased by drovers were driven on to the major tryst at Falkirk.

The Highland cattle I saw in the field near Coylumbridge were doubtless very placid because there was no pressure upon them. Seeing a beast occasionally lumber from one choice area of pasture to another, I tried to imagine 1,000 other beasts like it, confined to a road and its immediate verges, being pressed— but not too sternly—by attendants and their dogs. In the crisp, autumn air, the accumulated vapour from the nostrils of many beasts would give the impression that the drove was steaming. In dry weather, dust would be kicked up from the unmetalled road at every footfall. There would be scents never known in

Araby—the pungent, cloying scent of excited cattle, and the tang of their droppings.

When Bishop Forbes arrived at Dalwhinnie in the August of 1723 he watched West Highland cattle, reared on the islands, moving southwards after crossing the Corrieyairack. There were eight droves—1,200 beasts in all—and their destination was the tryst at Crieff.

The drovers (noted the Bishop) were well organised with "four or five horses with provisions for themselves by the way, particularly blankets to wrap themselves in when sleeping in the open air, as they rest on the bleak mountains, the healthy moors, or the verdant glens, just as it happens, towards the evening. They attend their flocks by night and never move until about eight in the morning and then march the cattle at leisure that they may feed a little as they go along. They rest a while at midday to take some dinner and so let the cattle feed and rest as they please."

The true drovers were something more than 'bullock-wallopers'. Some of them became quite wealthy through trading in cattle. They employed lesser men to drive the beasts. Bishop Forbes related: "The proprietor does not travel with the cattle but has one for his deputy to command the whole and he goes to the place appointed against the day fixed for the fair."

Alas, the Bishop—like many other travellers who left us their impressions of the trade—was not well versed in judging stock. The fascination for me lies in the animals themselves—tough animals with as much a right to the hill grazings as the deer. James Macdonald, who wrote *General View of the Agriculture of the Hebrides* in 1811, knew the kyloe well. He left us a description of the type of cattle which the folk of mainland Scotland saw in vast numbers on their journey from the distant islands to the dinner tables of England. Macdonald's description is almost a prose poem:

A bull of the Kyloe breed should be of a middle size, capable of being fattened to fifty stone avoirdupois. His colour should be black (that being reckoned the hardiest and most durable species), or dark brown, or reddish brown, without any white or yellow spots. His head should be rather small, his muzzle fine, his eyes lively and prominent, his horns equable, not very thick, of a clear, green and waxy tinge; his neck should rise with a gentle curve from the shoulders, and should be small and fine where it joins the head; his shoulders moderately broad at the top, joining full to his chine and chest backwards, and to the vane of his neck forwards.

His bosom should be open, his breast broad, and projecting well before his legs; his arms, or fore thighs, muscular and tapering to his knee; his legs straight, well covered with hair, and strong boned. His chine or chest should be so full as to leave no hollows behind the shoulders; the plates strong, to keep his belly from sinking below the level of his breast. His back or loin should be broad, straight and flat; his ribs rising above one another in such a manner that the last rib should be rather the highest, leaving only a small space to the hips or hooks; the whole forming a roundish, barrel-like carcass. His hips should be wide placed, rounded or globular, and a very little higher than the back.

His quarters (from the hip to the rump) should be long and tapering gradually from the hip backwards, and the turls, or pot-pones, not in the least protruberant; his rumps close to the tail; his tail itself should be thick, bushy, well-haired, long, and set on so high as to be in the same horizontal line with his back.

Indeed, "his general appearance should combine agility, vivacity and strength; and his hair should be glossy, thick and vigorous, indicating a sound constitution and perfect health".

Not all the black cattle of the Highlands moved southwards— one group, with attendant butchers, followed the military force led by Sir John Cope that was sent northwards to intercept rebels during the Jacobite upheaval. Cope abandoned his advance over the Corrieyairack to Fort Augustus when he became aware that a force of Highlanders was near. His ill-trained soldiers would be no match for the natives on their own steep and rocky ground. Over Corrieyairack, for centuries, passed the black cattle and their drovers, governed by commercial advantages rather than political strategy, moving in fair weather and foul.

Falkirk usurped Crieff as the setting of the main Scottish tryst.

Here, south of the Highland Line, were three main events a
year, the most important held in October. Thomas Pennant
(1772) was told that 24,000 head of Highland cattle were sold
at Falkirk annually, a number that rose to about 40,000 in the
early part of the following century and to 155,000 in the autumn
of 1850 when, incidentally, there were also over 200,000 sheep
and 4,000 horses.

The greatest drove routes in the north of England passed
through my native Yorkshire. Sometimes, while using a green
lane on the Pennines, I have tried to visualize the drovers—"a
rough, excitable set of men"—and their minions who stalked
along at between 10 and 12 miles a day. Their coarse, brown
plaids became blankets for the night. They subsisted, according
to Sir Walter Scott, on "a few handfuls of oatmeal and one or
two onions, renewed from time to time, and a ram's horn filled
with whisky". In the early days they were reimbursed at a
shilling a day—4s a day in the mid-nineteenth century. And
when the cattle had been delivered, the men had to undertake
a long walk home!

Inevitably, droving became redundant. There was a variety
of reasons for the decline: enclosure of the land across which
the droves had once been driven almost at will, new marketing
techniques and the transport revolution that sent railway trains
tooting into almost every corner of the land and enabled cattle
to be delivered to the markets without wear and tear. For years,
the Highland beasts had been specially shod against the rough-
ness of the roads they trod.

Yet English graziers still go to Scotland for outstanding beef
animals. I know one of them. He regularly delights me by
pasturing a group of Highland cattle in a field half a mile from
my home. When I contemplated the cattle near Coylumbridge,
it was not the novelty that absorbed me but the renewal of an
old acquaintance with what the writers of the Herd Book preface
proudly referred to as "the handsomest of our cattle".

8

AN ARCTIC WORLD

The road from Aviemore to Glen More, 'big glen', was a holidaymaker's road—fast and smooth. It led me to a forest park; then, by a series of zigzags, to a car park as large as a football field. From near the orderly rows of vehicles I was borne by chair lift to within easy walking distance of the summit of Cairn Gorm: an austere world of smooth, pinkish granite, moss and lichen.

I vowed that the next time I climb Cairn Gorm it will be by the old path, not the chair lift, despite the latter's obvious utility. The path is not gruelling. Generations of climbers have beaten out a way on the easiest gradients. Walking up the hill gives time for reflection. Using it, a visitor can condition himself to the change from lowland pine forest to high plateaux—from 800 to 4,000 feet above sea level.

The comparative isolation of Glen More ended when the modern road was laid. Once this was private—almost holy—ground, and in residence for most of the year were two deerstalkers, a gardener and a housekeeper, denizens of the big house and cottages, guardians of a glorious wilderness. Now it is one of the most crowded areas in the Highlands.

In Glen More, the Stewarts of Kincardine hunted the deer, and later it was a preserve of the Kings of Scotland. Glen More belonged to the Dukes of Gordon from the seventeenth century until, in 1923, it passed into its present ownership, the Forestry Commission. The Duke who reigned late in the eighteenth century kept up the diversion of falconry; he had several fine hawks, some of which had hatched out from eggs laid in Glen More. During the nineteenth century the economic life of the estate reflected that of most big Highland holdings. Sheep were here in number from 1831 until 1859, when it reverted to deer forest.

What was once a private road leading to the residence of a single land-owning family is now the broad, asphalted way to a forest park. Tourists co-exist with commercial timber in an area of nearly twenty square miles. Entering Glen More from Aviemore I crossed the floor of Speyside and was soon motoring between banks of impassive conifers. One tract of country had been blighted by fire. Now it was empty, tousled with pioneer grasses, and looking like Macbeth's blasted heath.

Flying across the semi-charred waste was a hooded crow (*feannag*), the northern variety of the carrion crow, which it resembles in shape, size and characteristics. The 'hoodie', with grey and not black feathers on parts of its body, appeared to have donned a lightly-toned cardigan especially for northern climes!

I had coffee and freshly-baked scones at a café overlooking caravans, pines and Loch Morlich. I had already seen the loch from a better angle, framed by Scots pines, edged to the east by golden sand piled up by the waves, and with the Cairngorms blocking out a quarter of the sky beyond. The Cairngorms looked far less impressive than they really are, lacking severe angularities.

Later, using a footpath at the lochside, I looked over two miles of water on which boats scurried like brightly-coloured water beetles. Some drake goosander floated in the quiet shallows. I listened, half hopefully, for the cheery whistle of the greenshank, which has long rejoiced in the swamps and heathered moors of Speyside. Now its numbers are few. A redstart, now more than halfway through its song period, broke the stillness. Later I heard, but did not see, a siskin—a bird which rears its young on the seeds of spruce and larch.

In quieter days tales were told of Red Hand, a tall and beefy

Highlander in spectre form, complete with battle gear. The sandy shore of Loch Morlich was his special haunt, and he held out a blood-spattered right hand.

Elizabeth Grant, a local commentator at a time when the Speyside forests were less well-known than they are today, told us of intrusions beginning in the seventeenth century, when men began the large-scale clearance of pines. The branches were lopped off and 'the trunks hauled by horses to the sides of burns and lochs like Morlich. Here the pines were peeled, allowed to dry out, and then set afloat to await a suitable time when they might be sent down the Spey to the seaside.

The lumbermen lived in bothies set up by the river, and large areas were denuded of timber. No serious replanting was undertaken, but in due course a benevolent nature somewhat replaced the eighteenth- and nineteenth-century despoliation. Then the attack on the forest was renewed, this time during world wars when there was a desperate need for raw materials like timber. A light railway linked up the forest with the Highland Line at Aviemore.

The average visitor, reading books about the Highlands, feels frustrated when he does not see the exotic birds and beasts so vividly noted in prose and picture. I have trudged for miles in the Highlands and seen only a meadow pipit. The visitor to Glen More has some compensation, for at Badaguish, in the Queen's Forest, the Forestry Commission has opened a wildlife park. Some distinctive creatures are always on view.

Those who book a trip to Badaguish in advance are provided with transport. There is a roughish ride along one and a-half miles of forest road, surrounded by everlasting conifers. I was thankful for the vehicle's canvas hood, for it was raining. Every tree dripped water. In the dull conditions the lichen plating on many a conifer tree stood out with vivid clarity.

At Badaguish I saw a red deer hind that had been brought from one of the Scottish islands. Its companion, a young stag, stayed shyly among the pines at the far side of the paddock. A badger could be viewed from a special platform overlooking the enclosure in which a wooden box had been sunk six feet as a sett, but the badger had preferred to make its own hidey-hole and ignored the box. 'Badgie' was living happily at about 1,500 feet above sea level, which is rather higher than the norm in the Highlands. It was conditioned by regular feeding to appear when visitors were likely to be present.

One of the trails in Glen More leads from near the Lodge and runs north-easterly to cross the pass of Ryvoan with, ultimately, a zigzag descent into the valley of the Nethy and the Seafield lands of Abernethy. The route took me high enough to feel a sense of special companionship with the Cairngorms and to have a vantage point for viewing Speyside. Pines dotted the slopes in a rocky gorge.

The weather steadily improved. Where pines were plentiful, goldcrests gave their thin, hard calls which a friend compares to the whirring of a diminutive sewing machine. There were, inevitably, a few coal tits. A spotted flycatcher darted at winged insects dancing in shafts of sunlight. The bird life was interesting but, on this day, not profuse. There might be many more birds in sight in October, when some of the immigrant thrushes from Scandinavia—fieldfares and redwings—have a landfall on the shores of Moray Firth and use the line of Ryvoan on their way further south. Skeins of grey geese have also been seen sweeping grandly by.

What remains of a cottage, standing at the crossing of ancient ways, is now used as a bothy—one of the invaluable little shelters of the Cairngorm area. It has not been regularly inhabited for over a century, degenerating into a single-roomed shack. The annual meeting of the Mountain Bothies Association in 1971 was told of its plight. "The door is shaky and the sheep get in!" stated a subsequent report. "Only a quarter of the flooring remains—the rest is earth and stones. Whether burnt deliberately or accidentally, it is hard to say. What is left is at least sound, while that which is gone was semi-rotten." Plans were made to renovate the surviving section in 1972.

Back in mainstream Glen More, I motored to the gravelly car park near the chair lift, gaining about 1,000 feet in altitude with no physical effort beyond operating the car's gears, clutch and brake. A yellow hammer had involuntarily made the journey. Struck by a car at much lower level, it was now simply a dishevelled corpse lodged in the vehicle's radiator.

The souvenir shop at the chair lift was selling 'cairngorms'—quartz crystals, semi-precious, that are usually found in veins. The crystals that littered the surface have long since been picked up and cashed. Brown is the commonest hue, but some stones are brighter, more interesting, the hues ranging from yellow to black. Though associated with the Cairngorms by name, they are found elsewhere, even in England. John Grant of Ryvoan found a 50-pound stone on Ben MacDhui and gave it to Queen Victoria, who paid him £50 for it. The old-timers panned the local streams with all the zest of the Forty-Niners, but their trade suffered—as did that for other British minerals—when foreign imports provided an unfair competition because they could be mined at much less cost.

The chair lift is three-quarters of a mile long, and in two stages provides an effortless journey up the hill for another 1,000 feet. There was a lulling effect. I had the notion of floating in a vacuum except when the chair jerked a little on nearing a pylon. A local man warned me to don extra clothing when ascending Cairn Gorm, and it has been calculated that the temperature decreases 1 degree Fahrenheit with each passing 300 feet. The day was calm and warm, and if there was a change of temperature with increasing altitude I was unaware of it.

So I ascended, feeling during this silent, floating journey as an astronaut must feel as he whirrs around the earth. There was such a sense of detachment that I could look hard, long and objectively at the range ahead—or, at least, a goodly part of the northern side of the Cairngorms. The whole range extends over 300 square miles. Guide books in my rucksack had informed me that the range takes its name from the Cairn Gorm, which means 'blue hill'. This is not the highest point, the distinction going to Ben MacDhui. To confuse the issue a little further, the Gaelic name of the range is Monaruadh, meaning 'red mountains'—an allusion, no doubt, to the pink fellspar contained in the granite. Across the valley of the Spey lay those grass hills, the Monadhliath, which are mainly composed of schist as opposed to granite, and this name means 'grey mountains'. Robert Gordon, a Scottish geographer in the seventeenth century, named features of the Cairngorm range "Carn-gorum, Bini-bourd, Bin-Avion and Bin-vroden".

Distant hills were delicate studies in grey and white—the grey from rocks whose reflective qualities were not being tested, there being a light mist, and the white representing remnant patches of snow. Cracks and crannies, ledges and corries, were streaked with snow, and it reminded me to look out for snow buntings— sparrow-sized birds of amazing stamina and cheerful disposition. There are wintering flocks of birds that nest in Greenland and Scandinavia, and some groups of buntings are seen on the car park below the chair lift, where they dine on tit-bits of food discarded by visitors.

The snow buntings of most interest to naturalists are the few —a very few—that remain here, at the southern part of their immense nesting range, to breed. These birds choose the highest places, invariably above 3,000 feet, the cocks singing in the echo-chambers of the high corries and the females tucking their nests away under jumbled rocks. Few nests are found. Desmond Nethersole-Thompson, an authority on snow buntings, found only 38 nests in more than 30 years, during which he camped on the high hills for a total of 265 nights.

He is one of the most recent of a class of intrepid naturalists for whom a quest for nests has incurred incredible cost in effort and discomfort. An early seeker of buntings was John Young, who discovered the first nest with eggs in mainland Scotland in 1888. John Woolley, another Victorian, provided us with some early observations of nesting birds, writing that "presently the cock flew away to a distance of 200 yards and settled on a rock, sometimes flying up and into the air and emitting its short but melodious warble. The hen took a sweep around the hill, alighting among the stones about 100 feet above us". Ornithologists who have sought the snow bunting can fill in many details of the setting: remote, sterile, often wind-swept. Such brief observations might follow years of toil in uncomfortable places.

The first snow bunting nest to be discovered on the Cairngorms had been made on Ben Avon. The bird built at about 3,700 feet above sea level, and the nest and eggs now repose in the British Museum. The Royal Scottish Museum has the nest and eggs of a Scottish snow bunting, collected in 1910 by the brothers Blackwood. Their efforts were arduous in the extreme, rendering them "almost too tired to speak". The men travelled overnight from Edinburgh to Aviemore, reaching Loch an Eilein just before 5 am. It was 17 hours before they returned to the loch, during which time they had slogged into the wilds, carrying much equipment, including heavy cameras.

There were no snow buntings to be seen during the ascent of Cairn Gorm—nor, in reflection, was a sighting probable. The most cheerful sound was the zit, zit of a dipper following the line of a stream. My chair was in position over the water as the bird flashed along this stretch and I looked directly down on it, seeing its dark back and wings but not, from this angle, the white bib. The dipper, bird of rushing burns, has been found nesting at 4,000 feet on the Cairngorms. As it curtseys on a mid-stream boulder, the white bib looks like a fleck of foam. When the dark feathers have caught the eye of the sun they are revealed as dark brown, not black, as many suppose.

The dipper scutters about the beds of burns when collecting food, and thus it exploits a food niche not shared by other British birds. Once it was slaughtered as a pest on good fishing grounds, and Ritchie relates that a Speyside man who killed a dipper during the angling season was given the right to fish with a rod in the close season!

More and more snow was revealed during the second stage of the chair lift journey. That year the remnant patches would be replenished in June and July. There was an August fall in 1727, and doubtless snow has descended in high summer on many occasions. In November of the year of my visit tragedy overtook a school party as a blizzard of great fury produced a 'white out', air blending with the snow and blotting out the scene.

I was looking across hills that once were remote, little visited, but are now known to the world and his wife, who have such easy access to Cairn Gorm. I beheld the highest range of hills in Britain whose distinctive wildlife is being preserved for prosterity. For in July 1954, part of the Cairngorm area was declared a National Nature Reserve. Added to in 1963 and 1966, mainly through agreement between the Nature Conservancy and several landowners, it now covers just on 100 square miles.

Slowly, smoothly, I was conveyed into an Arctic world. I travelled beyond the heather moors and their stock of red grouse to the haunts of the ptarmigan. The day remained untypical of the Cairngorms. I noticed no real difference in temperature in the final 2,000 feet. It had been an extraordinary winter. During the previous spring, a Yorkshire friend crunched snow underfoot as he plodded from the head of the chair lift to the summit of Cairn Gorm; he photographed a ptarmigan perched on one of the chair lift buildings. When I trod on Cairn Gorm, the pinkish rocks were mainly clear of snow; they were dry, dusty indeed, and the mini-vegetation had been browned by prolonged drought. I moved in an arid area. Just over the hill, half a dozen skiers were enjoying one of the few remaining large patches of snow.

The scene was austere—an Ice-Age Britain, testifying to the abrasive power of ice sheets. For roughly a million years almost all Britain was subjected to periodic glaciation, with warmer periods in between during which creatures and plants of a temperate zone could establish themselves, to be swept away when next the ice moved in. There remained on the highest land a few species of the arctic-alpine type.

Ice moving down old river valleys gouged and deepened them, moulding the valleys into a distinctive U-shape. Ice removed sharp edges, polished the landscape, plucked out corries, and finally melted to leave layers of boulder clay. I looked out across Spey valley, then lowered my eyes to take in Loch Morlich, which occupies the place where a huge piece of ice melted and a 'kettlehole' was formed.

Up on the Cairngorms it was possible to picture the scene as it might have been when the ice had gone—to ponder on the long, chilling winters, lingering springs, short and hot summers and autumns nipped off by the returning winters. The silence would be broken, as now, by the springtime flurry of nesting birds pouring in from the south. The ptarmigan would be here, though, as it is today—a tough, all-the-year-round resident. The snowy owl would cross the tundral scene—as it has crossed the Cairngorms in recent times, a bird having been seen on Ben MacDhui. The reindeer would be here, grazing on lichen, between the tundral willows, and this fine beast has also been reintroduced.

My path to the summit of Cairn Gorm had been beaten out by the feet of thousands of ramblers. Here the rocks were smoother, more evenly laid, than those on either side. The way was also well-marked so that it would be clear to follow in snowtime or mist.

I slipped off a jersey as my forehead beaded with perspiration, and I remembered other Cairngorm journeys, when the wind threatened to blow me inside out and water coursed down my neck and back as the savage rain gained entry beneath my clothes. When winds batter these 300-million-year-old rocks, even standing is an effort. The wind, said a young climber I met on the way to the summit of Cairn Gorm, can be so strong you can see it.

And what storms! Edward T. Booth, a seeker of rare birds, was not an emotional man given to wild exaggeration. He was on Ben MacDhui in July 1876, when "mist and cloud rolled lower down the hill while the rain drifting in blinding showers rendered it impossible to advance . . . terrific gusts now and then dislodged pieces of slab and rock that went rolling down the side of the hill. Some of these passed us at no mean distance." These conditions were experienced in summer!

This strange primeval world is frequently misty. The mist—cold, damp, depressing—can hang about for days, even weeks. The Cairngorms have that hill country phenomenon known as the 'glory', when the shadow of a person is dramatically projected by sunshine on to rolling banks of vapour. The Great Grey Man (*Fear Liath Mor*) patters across the top of Ben

MacDhui where, incidentally, snow lies for about 200 days in the year.

Were lemmings present on the high Cairngorms? And did they give rise to stories about the *famh*—"a little ugly monster" with head "twice as large as his whole body beside"? There was a reference to the *famh* in 1794, when it was said to emerge from its lurking places on summer mornings, leaving a deposit of glutinous substance on the grass. A horse that ate the affected grass would surely die. A writer in 1841 gave the haunt of the *famh* as "the summits of the mountains around Glen Alvin, and no other place in the world that I know of. . . . He is only seen about the break of day, and on the highest verge of the mountain."

These hills might have been fashioned for romance and mystery. My map indicated Marquis' Well, said to lie at 150 feet from the summit and close to Margaret's Chest, a hollow named after a shepherdess who kept 'cairngorms' here. Another story relates that Margaret became mad while wandering on these hills, to which she had fled after being jilted by a Macintosh of Moy, and the name for the hollow should really be Margaret's Coffin.

I paused to rest, and rough-read a brochure about the Cairngorms. There would be a near-certainty of seeing a soaring eagle. Or maybe I would watch a peregrine falcon stooping after prey. The blue or mountain hare would frolic almost at my feet.

There was no eagle. No peregrine. No blue mountain hare— though I would have expected to find a hare lower down. Its blue tinge is the effect of lighter, greyish tips to the brown pelage in summer and autumn. The high-lying hares are white in winter and, like the ptarmigan, have three moults every year.

After trudging around the highest parts of the Cairn Gorm I was prepared to settle for a wheatear in the absence of other birds. The cock bird, with its plumage toned black, white and grey, is less conspicuous on the high, rocky Cairngorms than in any other place I know. A wheatear did appear in due course. It was a cock in song flight, rattling harshly. I saw a bumble bee and a meadow pipit. The bird circling high above was not an eagle resting on a thermal but a great black-backed gull. Lower down, perched beside a snow drift, was a raven, something of a novelty in an area where sheep are not common and there is a limited amount of carrion.

So I strode, a little disappointed, in the shadowless wilderness of granite and tiny plant life. The views were sublime and compensated for the paucity of birds and beasts. Due south, but just out of sight until I moved away from the cairn, lay Loch Avon, and at the head of it the Shelter Stone, where the Wolf of Badenoch is said to have taken cover. The loch, lapping and fretting at an altitude of 2,600 feet, is over a mile long and its overspill forms a tributary of the Spey.

I thought of royal visitors to Ben MacDhui. Queen Victoria and Prince Albert ascended from their Highland base in Deeside, the Queen on the back of a pony, in 1859. She recorded in her journal that "we ascended very gradually, but became so enveloped in mist that we could see nothing—hardly those just before us! Albert had walked a good deal; and it was very cold." At the summit, the mist was dispersed by a breeze and Victoria saw the "grandest, wildest scenery imaginable." Gladstone climbed Ben MacDhui, on foot, in 1884.

On the day I reached the top of Cairn Gorm without puffing, the best of the floral display was yet to come from plants which exist because they extend root systems well below the ground to reach an area that is constantly moist. J. Grant Roger has stated that most of the 75 British arctic-alpine species occur in the Cairngorms. There is beauty in miniature for those who are prepared to bend their backs and intently regard a plant life that keeps low. In June, carpets of creeping azalea and the moss campion give a rust-red sheen to these high places. The former is red, the latter pink, and with other hilltop plants they combine colourfully to off-set the Cairngorm starkness.

I looked twice at a small boulder lying at the rim of the plateau; it took a little time to realize that this 'boulder' was different because it was covered with feathers. I had located a cock ptarmigan! Here was a bird about the size of a red grouse but much more interesting to me because I had seen the species

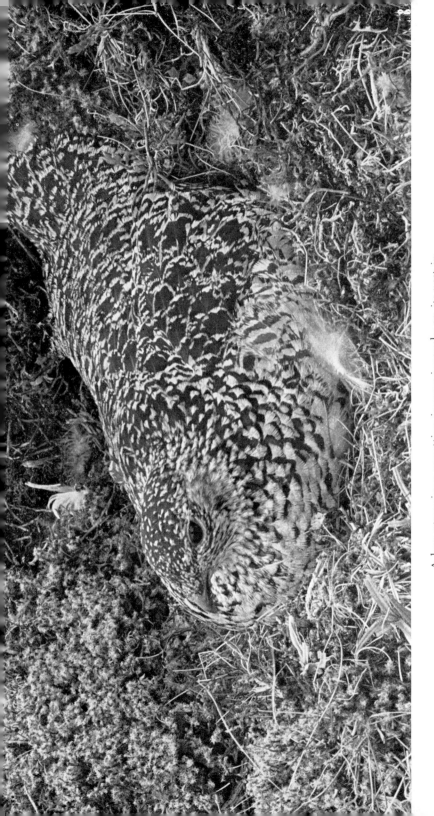

A hen ptarmigan squatting inconspicuously on its nest in Arctic Scotland

Woodcock on its nest in a Highland deciduous wood; its lowered head shows that it is aware of being seen

Recumbent roe kids. The further one has not yet dried after birth

infrequently. The ptarmigan sets the stamp on the Arctic character of the Cairngorms. It is the only bird of the Arctic tundra that breeds commonly in our land.

In view was a typical grouse—small head, short but curved beak, plump body, long tail—but a bird that inhabits regions where the much commoner red grouse would doubtless perish. On the Cairngorms, the territories of ptarmigan girdle the hills between roughly 3,000 feet and 3,800 feet, not specifically on the plateaux. Adam Watson, who has studied them with care over many years, noted their main food: shoots, leaves and the green stems of crowberry, blaeberry and heather, with some dwarf willow and other plants.

My ptarmigan stretched out its neck to an incredible length and surveyed me statuesquely, resembling a long-necked wine bottle. The plumage was that of early summer, mainly grey and white, with a vermillion wattle that screamed to be noticed. Ptarmigan (in Gaelic, *tarmachan*) is a sub-species of a bird found around the chilly top of the world. About twenty-two races have been described, and it was appropriately a Scot, William Macgillivray, who in 1837 first noted the difference between the Highland race and those on the Continent.

There was no physical barrier to keep the ptarmigan in its prescribed Cairngorm haunts, but it was imprisoned as surely as if someone had found a means of preventing it from leaving them. Such is the price of specialization. The bird I saw in the warmth of a May afternoon had, a few weeks before, with other ptarmigan, been roosting in caves scraped out of snow or facing a howling, icy wind, without flinching. Its three-times-a-year moult enables it to escape detection by its enemies. This tough hill bird also annually sheds and renews its claws.

The change into winter plumage is apparently induced by falling light values. The moult goes on slowly, but white is fairly general from October onwards. Winter's feathers are thicker than those of the summer, giving the ptarmigan the maximum insulation; even the feet have special protection, being feathered to the claws. Feathering on the pads of the toes will enable the ptarmigan to take a good grip on snow.

G

The ptarmigan was about 40 yards away when I first became
aware of it. My slow, devious approach made the bird uneasy.
At 30 yards it scrambled on to a boulder, jerking its wattled
head, standing very erect. I went nearer, and the ptarmigan
waddled a little but was still disinclined to fly, shuffling between
boulders. Ptarmigan tend to be as calm or as wild as the prevail-
ing weather.

Suddenly the bird was up and away, white wings moving
rapidly. The wings stopped beating as the bird went along the
rim of the hill at great speed. A curious sound was to be heard:
a dry 'grackle'.

Pairing takes place in April, even before the snowfields have
cleared. Now the birds would be territorially-minded, and I was
confident that my ptarmigan had not gone far. It had merely
belched its disapproval—as indeed cocks do to each other when
dawn comes early, greyly, to these hills.

Snow does not keep to regular seasons on the Cairngorms. If
there is much new snow when the eggs have been laid, a hen
ptarmigan may have to abandon the nest. Normally, the bird
sits hard, being cryptically-coloured, not only keeping the eggs
from the gaze of predators but protecting them from the
frosts.

The ptarmigan that allows itself to be stroked is not 'tame' as
humans know it—the bird is using a defensive stratagem of great
ancestry. Ptarmigan have actually been lifted from nests and,
apart from kicking their legs, have remained still, limp, until
replaced. The chicks, almost instantly active, snap up insects
and are trying out their wings when they are less than a fortnight old. They are as precocious as the chicks of the red
grouse.

Colonel Thornton enjoyed the company of ptarmigan. He
speculated about their ancestry. "I have remarked, though no
great botanist, that all flowers of the same plant, on the tops of
mountains, are similar to those found on the edges, except being
whiter and smaller, according to the height they are found on;
and I am confident it is so with respects to game: I am, therefore, of the opinion that ptarmigants are moor-game, stinted

in their growth, and varying in their colour from local situation only."

Charles St John, master sportsman in the Victorian tradition, commented in 1846 about the ptarmigan's confiding ways. The ptarmigan (not the Cairngorm birds in this case) "are seldom at all shy or wild but, if the day is fine, will come out from among the scattered stones, uttering their peculiar croaking cry, and running in flocks near the intruder on their lonely domain. . . . When the weather is windy and rainy, the ptarmigan are frequently shy and wild; and when disturbed, instead of running about like tame chickens, they fly rapidly off to some distance, either round some shoulder of the mountain, or by crossing some precipitous and rocky ravine, get quite out of reach".

Thus, concluded St John, "the shooting of these birds should only be attempted on fine, calm days. The labour of reaching the ground they inhabit is great, and it often requires a firm foot and steady head to keep the sportsman out of danger after he has got to the rocky and stony summit of the mountain".

I followed my cock ptarmigan along the edge of Cairn Gorm, walking part way down a moderate slope, using the slabs of granite as stepping stones, slipping only when I had my attention claimed by the spectacle of rounded, snow-streaked hills stretching off to misty horizons. I soon located the bird and watched it waddle away, breast close to the ground, uplifted tail edged by black.

Once again the crackling call was to be heard. The sound came from lower down the slope, where another cock bird was displaying. It rose with a loud, belching call. Then it seemed to rest against the wind, croaking. The ptarmigan was still calling as it dived, white wings decurved and rigid as though the muscles had locked.

I heard a deep croak ahead, and saw a ptarmigan go behind a rock. Only the wattled head and neck appeared in view as, in due course, the bird showed itself again, surveying me from behind boulders, then shuffling to an outcrop to sit and stare 25 yards away. This ptarmigan was restless and, giving a hoarse rattle, it launched itself over the edge to disappear from view along the rim of Cairn Gorm.

Later, two other birds followed the ridge, skimming the ground. They were only 30 feet up but moved out to travel hundreds of feet above a litter of boulders on the side of a deep glaciated valley.

Having had light refreshments at a circular café named after the species I had just seen, I decided to walk off the hill. At about 2,000 feet above sea level, a red grouse called: *go-bak, go-bak*. The call of the 'moorcock' inspired a Gaelic cry: *Co, co, co, mo chlaidh, mo chlaidh*. It has been translated as 'who, who, who, my sword, my sword'.

This cock bird had just come into full summer plumage, and its podgy body was chestnut-red, dark in hue, barred with black. I beheld one of the glamour birds of Scotland, in a quest for which the sportsman (or, more frequently now, sportsmen, for syndicates are the rule) might pay up to £7,000 a year.

Here is a variety, in island Britain, of the willow grouse— internationally a widespread race. The willow grouse is mainly white in winter, but in the long, slow, highly selective process of evolution what is now the red grouse adapted itself to a situation where the lower hills it frequented were no longer snow-clad for long periods, even in winter. What we have, in effect, is a dark-toned race of willow grouse.

Colonel Thornton admired the toughness of the red grouse, which he referred to as "moor game". These birds did not seek out lower land when "dreadful storms" blasted the hills. The Colonel observed: "In the winters of 1782 and 1783, a very creditable farmer assured me, moor-game fed among his cattle and fowls. They form flocks, as I am informed, of three and four thousand; but, as I never was, nor do I wish ever to be here in winter, I cannot pledge myself for the truth of this, any more than for many other Highland stories; but I believe it is very possible."

After the belching of ptarmigan, and the spluttering call of a red grouse, it was pleasant, during a second visit to the Cairngorms, to listen to the bird which is to the gorges of these

northern hills what the nightingale is to the copses of the South
Country. For me, the sweetest springtime song in wild country
is the clear, fluty whistling of the cock ring-ouzel.

I stood entranced as the ouzel song sounded in a confined
space. Then, with some effort, I isolated the bird from its vast
setting. It had used a rowan as its perch and its feathering looked
black, but is actually greyer on the wings. Black, that is, except
for the light crescent on its upper breast, which resembled a
quarter moon lying on its back. As I neared the bird it became
tense, poised on the edge of the branch, nervously twitching its
wings and tail, and no longer singing. It moved off with a sharp
alarm call, and was lost to sight among the rocks higher up the
gorge.

Generally, the ring-ouzel takes over where the blackbird leaves
off, but there is an overlap of the species here and there. Ring-
ouzels reach the Cairngorms in early April, and soon the cock
birds are in loud, clear song. The female is brown, its breast
crescent less well defined, and during my visit in late May there
could be some young birds in mud-lined nests. Some pairs
manage to raise two broods in the season.

Ring-ouzels slip away inconspicuously, many of them by
night, having dined liberally on the berries of rowan, cranberry
and bilberry. When the winter blizzards sweep across the Cairngorms, birds from this area are wintering in North Africa.

9

VALLEY OF THE GOATS

I heard a man of Carrbridge say "Slochd". If I had not asked him specially to pronounce the odd name I might have thought that he was simply clearing his throat. Slochd lies near the A9 about 20 miles south of Inverness. It means 'valley of the wild goats'.

Look at a coloured map and you will see that the area north of Carrbridge is blotched with the browns that signify high land. It is generally high and desolate but without jutting rock turrets or hills with the conspicuous pyramidical form that visitors bring to mind when imagining mountain country. Apart from Slochd, there are few conspicuous crags. Slochd gives a touch of Highland grandeur to what is otherwise a tract of desolate moorland.

Pleasant Carrbridge gives no hint of the bleakness of the moors to the north, though the countryside round about has not been totally subjugated by man. The bridge featured in the name of the village was built in 1717 and is now just a curiosity. This Old Bridge of Carr, an arch with no parapets, gives the impression of a rainbow set in stone.

The road from Carrbridge rises fairly gently, as befits a major route. It passes through moorland and beside relatively small plantations of pines. The trees off-set but do not challenge the general austerity. A gamekeeper told me that on a late winter day—a day of thawing snow, which gave the landscape a piebald look, also notable for "a wee bit o' sun"—he entered one of the plantations and observed a small flock of crested tits.

The moors, then, are the dominating feature, and coming from the Yorkshire Pennines I felt at home as I trod across them. When following a byroad I saw hares, not the common brown hares which I regularly see springing from forms set in reeds, but the blue or mountain hare. Now that spring was here, the hares were patchy white, well on in the process of moulting. Hares are nervous, excitable at normal times; now, with spring fever upon them, some fast and erratic chases were taking place.

A hoarse call, *pruk*, deflected my attention to the sky, where a raven was passing over. Other moor sounds were the crowing of a cock grouse, distant burbling call of a curlew, and the call of the golden plover—the short, sad, soulful whistle of a cock bird on its territory. A week or two later a friend, visiting this same area, found some dainty plover chicks.

In a wasteland of undulating moors and crags, Slochd is a stupendous feature—a deeply-cut gorge with the crags rising impressively, like a Nevada backdrop in a western. There is nowhere in the immediate area where an interested traveller can park his car. The road dips and bends. There are traffic barriers beside it. A driver snatches a glimpse of soaring rocks and then, if he is in a similar plight to myself, he does not loiter. I had five tons of lorry pressing me from behind!

After opting out of the traffic race at the first opportunity, I returned on foot to the 'valley of the goats'. The crags looked lifeless. Not even a sheep trod the ledges, where cushions of spring grass made the rocks look less naked. Eventually I fixed my eye on the noble form of a billy goat. If this mainly white animal had not been standing, I would probably have overlooked it. Lowering my binoculars I scanned the Slochd with naked eyes. The form of the goat was indefinite like a patch of snow.

About 30 goats give meaning to the name Slochd. The goats are feral—domestic stock gone wild. They are unattended, seldom visited, rarely culled and, to my knowledge, not claimed by any specific person. Years ago some of the goats kept by crofters escaped; they made for the hills. Within a generation or two the goats had become truly wild. (Even domestic cattle can become too wild for man to handle in two years.) Now the goats belong to the crags and to the wild moorland by the right of many generations.

A shopkeeper at Carrbridge remembered when there were twice as many goats as today. Periodically a farmer gathered them up with his dogs. He slew some of the nannies and castrated the most undesirable billies. "Very little of a good nanny was wasted. The blood was used as a fertilizer for the gardens. Hides were sold to a maker of sporrans (presumably some of them to be borne by the Highland regiments), and if you'd got a decent pelt you'd cure it and use it as a rug."

The fat (there was not much fat) was rendered down and used as dubbin. Parts of the entrails were cleaned to be used for 'meallie pudding', a mixture of oatmeal, onions and fat. A billy's horns, usually heavily serrated, were used by the makers of walking sticks. "Goat meat tastes something like pork and is good enough if you're really hungry. A live billy can stink like blazes ! "

Because goats have not been regarded as beasts of the chase, there is no quaint and complex terminology, such as that surrounding deer or hawks. These Highland goats are mainly black or white. A local woman said that she occasionally saw two goats that were slatey-grey. "One has a horn curved backwards. The horns of the other goat stick out—just like bicycle handlebars."

There is nothing to stop a goat with wanderlust from moving out of the parish. A Grantown man who was motoring between Newtonmore and Laggan watched a group of goats grazing within 80 yards of the road. Goats, like other hill animals, tend to move up the slopes in summer to be free of the menace of buzzing or biting flies. They return to lower levels when the bad weather sets in, and they know the most sheltered places. The goats of Slochd lie up in caves in the rocks during prolonged snow, a habit evidenced by the way the green stuff round about is heavily cropped.

Travellers on the Great North Road are most likely to see

goats at Slochd in winter and spring, when the animals trip
lightly, fantastically, along ledges where sheep move at extreme
risk. Goats, indeed, were anciently kept to eat the grass in places
where a sheep might become cragfast. In blustery weather, the
goats tend to leave the exposed crags. They quest for the lee
side of the hill and, being very cautious, will work their way
round slowly, maybe covering miles of country.

Goats mate in the autumn, and unlike red deer there is no
segregation of the sexes outside the breeding season. Within a
group of goats there is a hierarchy, the lord of the herd being a
master billy which dominates the young billies and discourages
fraternization with the nannies as these come in season. King
Billy sometimes asserts his authority by fights following threat
displays. The structure of the herd is not unlike that of the
ancient park cattle.

Billies fight ferociously, and a man who watched such a tussle
told me that two goats were at the rim of a depression, the
dominant billy being 'upbank', repeatedly driving its rival into
the depths. A billy has its strong, repugnant smell mainly during
the breeding season.

There is a five-month gestation period and the kids are born
in January and February—a time hostile to young life. Many
kids perish in the hardest winters. The effects of unkind weather
are seen in spring and summer, when few if any young goats
are running with the nannies. Apart from being exposed to cruel
winds, rain or snow, the kids may be in desperate trouble through
the premature drying up of the nanny's milk supply.

It is pleasant, for those local people who care, to see kids
frolicking about the crags and on the moors following a mildish
winter. A gamekeeper who makes a spring tour looking for fox
earths told me of seeing kids sleeping in the sun. When a kid
is new-born, a nanny suckles it and then hides it away in coarse
vegetation. The gamekeeper remembered a day when he found
kids that were dozing, the rest of the herd having moved on.
Alarmed, the kids scampered after the others at impressively
high speed.

The billy I saw on the crags was a fine beast. The horns curved backwards, resembling those of an ibex. For the moment it was not obsessed with feeding. "Goats", I was told, "are shrub-eaters —browsers rather than grazers. They like the twiggy type of vegetation. They say a goat will eat anything. I prefer to think of it as an animal that doesn't stick fast in hard times. Then a goat takes anything that's remotely edible."

The goats are not exceedingly wild. "At times you can get fairly close to them—a matter of 40 yards. A red deer in the same circumstances would dash off into the next county." A new-born kid will—like some other young mammals—readily take to a human who finds it in its impressionable first hours. One kid followed a human across the moor. He could not escape from it!

Carrbridge had, until this visit, impressed me simply as a halt for refreshment—for myself and the car. Then a woman serving at the garage mentioned local birds and beasts. There had been a wild cat—one with a bushy, barred tail rather than just a domestic cat gone wild—which she had surprised while driving at night, the car headlamps making it blink before it scuttered away into cover. A gamekeeper in this district trapped 17 wild cats—and reckoned he had not accounted for a tenth of the local population.

Even more stimulating than talk about fauna was the visit I paid to Landmark, a comparatively new Highland centre, close to the A9, its car park being beaten out between high-standing Scots pines. The paths were the least obtrusive I have seen, and one of them led invitingly away, between pines, at the start of a nature trail.

A brochure I saw about Landmark made a visit irresistible. I might "walk through a crevasse into an exhibition and hear Arctic winds whistle overhead; experience the story of man's struggle to survive; see the animals that inhabited the country; grind my own oatmeal with a hand quern; and meet the Reverend Henry Throgmorton, collector of the last osprey egg". In Landmark's multi-screen auditorium I could be "involved for 20 minutes in a hundred centuries of Highland history".

What I remembered with especial pleasure was an evening

film show. The main film was about Speyside wild life. We were transported to the High Cairngorms, and one sequence showed a dotterel chick running at furious speed, with twinkling legs, over a far-from-smooth terrain. We went to Loch Insh at flood-time, seeing the majority of wintering swans. Eventually, we were by the sea—a brisk sea, each wave capped with white foam —and observed the Spey forcing a way into the flow tide. With what success could be readily seen by the different tones of river and sea.

10

PLAIN OF THE GREAT PINES

Rothiemurchus is a name that thrills—and intrigues—me. Slight differences have occurred in the rendering of the Gaelic from which the name was drawn. I also noted three main derivations of that name: great fort of the pines, wide plain of the fir trees, or—and this pleased me most—the plain of the great pines.

Abernethy, Glen More and Rothiemurchus were the three great timber forests of Speyside. Yet for centuries before man imposed his will on the scenery, the pines lived their stately lives with roots extending far into the porous material left by glaciers and ice sheets, supplemented by later erosion from the hills.

The soils are rather poor. They do not yield a rich and varied flora, but here are ideal conditions for pines and their attendants: juniper and larch. And where the trees are thin on the ground grows some of the lustiest, most colourful heather in Scotland.

Colonel Thornton rendered the name "Rothemurcos" and commented that "this immense forest . . . is sufficient of itself to falsify the assertions of Churchill and all other writers, who have presumed to declare that there are no trees in Scotland". Rothiemurchus became disastrously thinned, unexpectedly its timber being used for water pipes in London during the latter part of the seventeenth century. The trunks were bored out at special mills here and in Abernethy.

Colonel Thornton dined at Rothiemurchus. He had hoped to meet "his Grace of Gordon", and of giving him thanks for the civilities shown me and my party; but some material business prevented him from coming. Mr Grant of Rothemurcos has built a very commodious house, not in the best situation, though his table &c is the most enviable in the world, as is his estate.

He was an acquaintance of mine when I was here before. As a proof that his table is well-served, I will only mention that he has added to every other luxury, what few possess, viz. roebucks, cairvauns, hare, black game, dottrel, white game, partridges, ducks and snipes; salmon, pike, trout, char, par, lampreys and eels, all of which are in abundance upon his estate.

Colonel Thornton tasted "some uncommonly fine char, fresh caught", which were superior to any he had tasted before. "They were absolutely a lump of fat," he enthused. "These fish, when fresh, have a taste something similar to that of a herring; a large pot of them Mr Grant was pleased to order to be sent me."

Rothiemurchus is almost a kingdom unto itself—a microcosm of the Highlands. Where it edges up to the river Spey there are oyster-catchers, *kleeping* over gravel bed and lush meadow. Rothiemurchus is in part a wild pine forest, and here during the late 1960s many hearts fluttered when that curious bird, the wryneck, little known in the north but still nesting in the south of Britain, was observed. There was not just one bird, nor even one pair, but several, and eventually the nests of three pairs were found. The birds were presumed to be of Scandinavian origin, deflected by easterly gales and finding suitable terrain in Strathspey.

There are, of course, crested tits, but in the pine forest I also heard the drumming of a great spotted woodpecker. Here nests the spotted flycatcher. The commonest bird in spring is undoubtedly the chaffinch, but here too can be heard willow warbler, coat tit, goldcrest and others.

The Rothiemurchus area is not all woodland. Hedge-bordered roads have scarcely outgrown their old duty as tracks for horses and carts. The roads wind and undulate, giving each car journey a sense of adventure. Follow the little roads, and Rothiemurchus unfolds its attractions like chapters within the covers of an exciting book. Where a road peters out, a well-beaten footpath takes over.

I saw stands of Scots pine, at the edge of which were hillocks raised by black ants. Beyond lay moorland—rank heather, a few red-barked pines, occasional grey stumps. This open country looked attractive—typically 'Highland' to many visitors—but was a mute memorial to the desecration that man can cause when he is insensitive to the natural order, or simply greedy.

Trees were cleared by fire or felling. Man's domestic stock prevented the natural regeneration of timber in what had been a well-wooded area. Later, grouse were encouraged—their numbers built up artificially high for sport. To provide fresh shoots for grouse and sheep, the heather was regularly burnt. What remains is virtually a monoculture. Ling crowds out most other plants, and in places the ever-spreading bracken sprouts and crowds out the ling.

There is rather more to it than ling. Cranberry, blaeberry, and the bearberry flower and fruit in profusion. On the high hills grows that delectable plant, cloudberry, its fruit like small strawberries. I knew an old Highlander who was obsessed by cloudberry and was ranting on about the plant as he died.

In damp areas, where the air is well flavoured by peat, nests the golden plover. Birds which are pasty-looking in winter, when black is absent from their plumage, return to the skirts of the Cairngorms looking smart in the nuptial dress of black and gold and white. Finding a nest is difficult. Even rarer is the sight of golden plover chicks, just dried off—little blobs of rich gold and black.

Scenically, this much-varied Rothiemurchus cannot be said to 'fizzle out'. Beyond the streams and lochans which give a sparkle to the uplands is the backdrop of the Cairngorms, which in spring are often grey, enveloped in light mist, a reliable sign of a thaw.

The local man who was my guide during a brief visit to Rothiemurchus divides his year between conducting pony treks and instructing aspirants in ski-ing. He keeps Welsh cobs for riding and told me that the world of pony-trekking is not all sunshine and serenity. There are climatic variations, and not a few days dawn grey and wet. Then there are times when either the horses or the people are irritable. On the day of our expedition, a lady trekker had withdrawn from the party just as the ponies settled down to their slow, plodding rhythm. He had to switch the ponies round—and it caused resentment among some of the animals. Every pony cherishes its position in the line. Even Welsh cobs have a pecking order!

On troublefree days he could settle back to enjoy an affinity with nature, travelling across country on the back of an animal that gained acceptance from the wild creatures. He had seen red squirrels scampering about the pines, their claws rasping on the bark, and had noticed gentle cascades of cone fragments being dropped by crossbills. Such pleasures are denied the people who travel by car, insulated from the world by metal and glass.

We turned right near Coylumbridge for Loch an Eilein. A tract of ground near the point of turning was pointed out as an old-time camping place of tinkers who had the sympathy of the Laird of Rothiemurchus. The Laird later changed his mind, and the tinkers had to move, for his word was law in these parts. When our journey was 200 yards old—and we began it by car— I braked to watch a red squirrel feeding 20 feet away. It sat on a grassed-over bank and held some unidentifiable substance with its forepaws, moving the object against its ceaselessly-champing teeth. What surprised me was that the squirrel had not carried the food to the heights of a tree before eating. I stared hard and long, having heard that the real old British stock of red squirrels, one of whose last haunts was the Highlands, is said to have a pelage of richer red than that of the introduced continentals.

The next stop was at a cottage where the old lady told us about her bird table, and more particularly about the visitors to it. In winter, the food—suet and not nuts—attracted crested tits. Immediately beyond the cottage were young pines that had been planted by man. They stood in an orderly fashion, each of about the same age as its fellows. I felt to be passing through a repository for telegraph poles!

The view opened out. Heather was banked on either side of a path that meandered and climbed between bushy heather. A buzzard circled. The low sunlight brought out the warmth of tone on its wings. When this area was almost continuous pine forest, the breeding birds included the goshawk, but it had become very rare as early as the eighteenth century. Goshawks have occasionally been reported from Speyside in recent years.

When the sight of a few trees and a glint of water marked out a lochan, I heard the vexed calling of a curlew. The bird's calls were short, sharp, not the lingering, bubbling call of a bird gliding around its territory. We were too far away to be the cause of its distress, so we looked for another source of danger. The curlew continued to call, its notes making the whole area ring with strident sound, and then a hooded crow was seen quartering the ground, undoubtedly looking for the curlew's nest.

The *Game Rearers' Annual* for 1903 had no good words for the 'hoodie', but acknowledged the bird's wily and intelligent nature. "Hooded crows are most difficult to destroy, and unless poison is used they cannot be successfully coped with," stated the anonymous writer. "Where poison is used, it is generally placed in the eyes of dead sheep, which usually provides a fatal lure to the hoodies."

We were striding out at about 1,000 feet above sea level. It was, said my companion, typical country for wild cats. He pointed to a line of crags composed of a dark face and jumbled boulders as an ideal lair for wild cats. The species is spreading again, mainly under cover of the new plantations. Wild cats, common early in the nineteenth century, were declared extinct in the locality by a Dr Forsyth writing in 1900. A Highland tom is an impressive beast, weighing about 15 pounds, and hefty and spiteful if roused. Here is a mammal of respectable ancestry in Britain that steadfastly refuses to have anything to do with man.

Roe deer—a doe—in winter pelage. The species is common in
Rothiemurchus

Mikel Utsi, who reintroduced the reindeer to the Scottish Highlands
and supervises a thriving herd on the slopes of Cairn Gorm

At Loch an Eilein we walked in shadow. Lingering sunlight lit up the island castle that marks out Loch an Eilein as something rather special in visual terms. A hard yellow light picked out details of the masonry with the clarity of lines on an etching, and the whole stood out conspicuously against conifers reduced by shadow to a dark amorphous mass. Beyond, rust-red where the sunlight caught them, were brooding hills.

How was the castle built? Did an islet exist here in the fifteenth century, when the oldest masonry was set in place? Or did ingenious man heap up material to provide an artificial base for the fortress? It has been claimed that a causeway leads to the castle and that stones forming the causeway were laid irregularly, to be unhelpful to strangers.

The beauty of Loch an Eilein stunned us into silence. We did not presume to test the old story that its castled islet returns a triple echo. The view was enough. Larches were ranged along the mainland shore. Birches crowded the slopes of Ord Ban. In view across the water were Scots pines that were saplings 250 years ago.

A common sandpiper trilled, and sped away, increasing its speed with jerky wingbeats, then gliding, dangerously near the water, wings stiff and angled downwards. The linnet-like notes of an unseen siskin came from the top of one of the larches, which had tasselly leaves. Resting on the walls of the castle were several red-breasted mergansers. We looked hopefully for an osprey, which occasionally arrives here on a fishing expedition. Ospreys nested on the ruined castle. There were none in sight that evening, but another buzzard floated by, broad wings turning upwards at the tips.

The ground near the conifers was sprinkled with cones. Some of them had been rifled for seeds. The half dozen we picked up had clearly been dropped by red squirrels, which was a disappointment. For the quest to Loch an Eilein was partly to see one of the bird celebrities of the Speyside forests that is observed fairly regularly here: the aptly-named crossbill.

No other British bird has crossed mandibles, and none has the colouring of the cock crossbill, which is reddish, accounted for

H

in Germany by a legend that a crossbill at the Crucifixion tried
to tear the nails from the cross and became soaked with blood.
In late May, family parties of crossbills may be seen, the young
being fed on seeds neatly extricated from cones.

Crossbills are indifferent to man but, living out their short
and hectic lives high above ground, on evergreens, they are not
easily seen. A commoner sighting for those who really look for
crossbills is that of fragments of rifled cones. The cock bird feeds
the brooding hen with pine seeds, and the nestlings—which
have straight bills—are provided with a diet of seeds during the
20 days before they have the strength and impulse to leave
the nest. Some do not succeed; they become food for red
squirrels.

I looked into the trees at Loch an Eilein until my eyes prickled,
but no crossbills showed themselves. Once, the twittering calls
of crossbills reached me from high above, but the birds were
already moving away.

Ornithologists discuss at length the origin and status of the
Scottish crossbill (*Loxia pytyopsittacus scotica*). Are the big-
beaked Scottish birds a distinctive local race—or a fairly recent
branch of a Continental race? Is the crossbill seen nesting on
Speyside a 'red' crossbill that has developed a specially large
beak, or does it belong to the race known as parrot crossbills?
The differences between the Scottish birds and those on the
Continent can be accounted for by an island race's long
separation from the main stock, though occasionally the common
crossbill (*Loxia curvirostra*) erupts into Britain from the North
European spruce forests. Sometimes the new immigrants mingle
with the native birds, but apparently they do not interbreed.
Common crossbills may remain to nest in Britain in southerly
areas, with East Anglia as a popular area. These birds often
choose roadside pines for their nests.

Man has long marvelled at the crossbill and the eccentricity
of its twisted mandibles. Matthew Paris, noting a crossbill
invasion in 1257, described the birds as "something larger than
larks, which ate the kernel of the fruit and nothing else, whereby
the trees were fruitless, to the loss of many. The beaks of these

birds were crossed, so that by this means they opened the fruit as if with pincers or a knife".

Making an evening visit to Loch an Eilein I was at least spared the attentions of black-headed gulls, for the day-shift of the wild was ending; less than half a dozen gulls stood around the car park. These gulls, dapper with their gleaming white feathers, chocolate-brown nuptial 'hoods' and scarlet bills, have the cheek of sparrows in a London park. On my last visit two gulls alighted on the bonnet of the car while I was still in the vehicle. During the day, every walk is punctuated by their raucous screams.

My companions and I had the Loch an Eilein nature trail to ourselves. We strode in the twilight, watched a roe deer bound from some lush grazings near the loch, and heard the gruff barking of roe from the woods. A tree-creeper shuffled up the rough bark of a pine like a streaky-brown mouse, and from somewhere near it came a high-pitched trilling call—the sound made by an excited crested tit.

Darkening woodland thrilled me, not only for what I saw—or tried to see—but by what I felt. There was an ageless atmosphere, a suggestion of an area unchanged and unchanging, though indeed nature is never still. Apart from the steady ageing process, and the supplanting of veteran trees by the thrustful young, the rhythm of the conifer woods is disturbed by sudden violence—by wind and fire.

In 1960 a number of veteran pines near Loch an Eilein were blown down in a storm. Colonel Thornton, visiting the loch in the eighteenth century—and calling it "Loch Neiland"— recorded that "immense fir trees were blown into all parts of the lake by heavy and very severe storms". He was absorbed by fishing, and the comments on trees were in relation to sport. "Beneath these old trees the fish [some monster pike] harbour and, running under or round them, few or none, I understood, have ever been taken by angling. What were killed had chiefly been shot."

Loch an Eilein still contains pike, which prey on the brown trout. Therefore this water contains a comparatively small number of good-sized trout, in contrast to the neighbouring

Loch Gamhna, which is pikeless and has a large number of fish whose average weight is smaller.

We walked in increasing gloom, passing a moist area where birch scrub and juniper co-existed with firs, the firs soaring as straight as ships' masts. In such an area there is an early flush of grass to tempt red deer. The deer also find shelter in bad weather, but they summer on the open hills.

As we approached Loch Gamhna, the barking of excited roe deer was heard less frequently. Gamhna is famous for its summertime display of water lilies but is not named after them. The name relates to stirks, young cattle—black cattle, no doubt —which were summered here, according to mainstream tradition, or had been driven to the shores of the loch by thieves, according to a local story. When the thieves heard the enraged owners approaching they tied stones to the horns of the cattle which were driven into the loch. The thieves were thus destroying the evidence of their guilt. Alas for them, when the owners arrived, and the thieves were protesting their innocence, one of the stirks, having struggled free of the stone, emerged shivering and dripping from the loch! Cattle thieves used a route near Gamhna to raid the richlands to the east, returning with droves of stolen cattle. The route they took is still known as 'thieves' road'.

Walkers with time to spare trudge up to Loch Einich. Colonel Thornton mounted an expedition to this area 200 years ago. He and his friends walked for three hours before reaching the loch, which

is said to be full of *char*, and on the cloudcapt mountains above are found *ptarmigants* (a species of white moorland game), *cairvanes* (a species of white hare) and some *dottrel*. We dined at possibly the coldest spring in the world, running most rapidly, and, had very good punch made with shrub, brought from Indereschy.

After resting a little, we proceeded, the attendants taking care, according to my former directions, that our cavalry should not eat. The pernicious quality of the grass, or bent, growing here, is a circumstance not exactly accounted for, but the horses, it seems, feeding on it, are absolutely poisoned. . . . This poisoning quality of the grass growing here, so fatal to horses, may possibly arise from its tufty, hard nature, which resembles a sponge; and, thus swelling in the stomach of the animal, like clover in cows, destroys it. . . .

Saw several broods of ptarmigants, but the rain, coming on suddenly, prevented our proceeding and we returned, after killing three brace and a half; the tercels killed the same number. They were much frightened at the hawks, which they must sometimes see, and their defence we found was, when pressed, to fly under the large loose rocks; so that we found some difficulty to retrieve them. Terriers really would be useful, for many we shall lose, when we come here to hawk, for want of them.

The party was soaked by rain, "but before my powder was quite wet, I contrived to kill a dottrel: had my powder from the first been dry, I could have killed at least seven or eight brace". He had seen almost all the ptarmigan ground in Scotland "but never saw above ten or a dozen in a day before, except in the farther parts of the Cairngorms, where they are tolerably numerous; but here they swarm".

We left Loch Gamhna with quickened pace, for the air had stilled; it was bitterly cold. Around us, the woodland had become a general dark mass in which it was hard to pick out the features of individual trees. The steel-grey Loch an Eilein lightened into silver in places touched by the last of the sun's afterglow. The silver was broken up into thousands of dazzling fragments in a small bay when a wigeon paddled away from patches of water lilies.

From the sky came three grunts, followed by a high-pitched *tissick*—the call made by a 'roding' woodcock. This bird engages in a territorial flight at dusk and dawn. I saw it in silhouette—a plump bird flying at about 40 feet, moving its wings slowly but positively and appearing to travel more quickly than the wing-beats suggested. The woodcock appeared to draw back its head at every *tissick*.

Charles St John, the Victorian sportsman of Morayshire, was the first man to describe in 1848 the woodcock's habit of carrying its young. I have never seen this happen, but a Lancashire naturalist who has, assured me it occurs occasionally. He had seen a woodcock bearing a well-grown but still flightless young and seeming to have some difficulty in remaining airborne.

A frog-like croaking occurred as two cock birds met at the periphery of a territory. The outraged bird flew close to the other, scolding it. The intruder was driven off, and the outraged bird resumed its roding, looking like a monster bat in the gloom.

11

ROE IN ROTHIEMURCHUS

Roe deer were grazing in the evening murk, and they looked as vague and insubstantial as shadows. The animals were spreading out across a large field of 'silage grass', having emerged from scrubland. Their blocky grey shapes were clear to see against the field.

These Rothiemurchus roe were grey because the sun had gone behind a bank of low cloud, giving a premature dusk, draining colour from the landscape. And now, in late May, the deer were still in greyish-brown winter coat. It would be thinning, however. Grey hair would fall or be rubbed away, and the roe would be seen wearing hair of reddish-brown (almost the colour of a lowland fox), with paler underparts.

Half a dozen heads were raised as the brakes of my car squealed a little. I had been driving on a hedge-bordered road at the western edge of the field, not in the least worried about tainting the air with obnoxious scents, for the evening was calm and rather cold.

When a deer lowers its head to feed, its visibility is reduced to a few feet. These roe deer were in thick grassland, and in the heads-down position could see only a few inches. They could confidently rely on the early warning devices of hearing and smell, but frequently stood and looked around.

For a time, my car became a mobile hide. I was relatively close to a young buck, and instantly recognized some of the main characteristics, which make it among the most attractive of mammals. The antlers were short in length, each horn having three points or tines. Because I beheld a young animal I could see its antlers were still in velvet, spring being the time when this hairy skin is cleaned off. I saw a short, rather blunt head, with dark marks near the muzzle resembling a drooping moustache. Scottish roe are said to be more grizzly about the face than those further south.

The roebuck moving gracefully on the floor of Spey valley was one of a species most widely distributed in Scotland. It is the smallest of our indigenous deer, but appearances can belie the facts. A mature roebuck can deal pugnaciously, even lethally, with rival deer at the time of the rut.

A roebuck being kept captive in the Lake District was confined by wire to a small corner of its normally big territory. It had to be content to watch while a pair of fallow deer roamed at will outside. In fact, the roebuck broke out of its temporary prison by lifting the wire netting with its antlers. Instantly it pursued the much larger fallow buck and spiked it neatly. The fallow died in the blink of an eyelid. The short but sharp horns of the roe had quested successfully for its heart.

In the Blair Atholl district they told of a man who was badly injured in exceptional circumstances. A roebuck being driven turned inexplicably on a line of beaters and the man was caught in the groin. He spent months in hospital.

Occupying a Highland dusk watching roe deer, I saw the representatives of a tribe that has survived lustily into an age when man has tipped the balance of nature well and truly in his favour and is often intolerant of his fellow creatures. The roe reached the Highlands many thousands of years ago in the wake of retreating ice. It was not among the first animals to return, spreading northwards with the spread of trees—of scrubby birch, then pine. Red deer, making an earlier entry, managed to reach Ireland before the collapse of the land bridge, but the roe was too late to follow them.

In their Scottish haunts, roe have survived innumerable changes in the landscape and the moods of man. In England, roe came close to extinction, but there were always good stocks in Scotland, and especially in Perthshire. A southern spread was possible in more enlightened times, aided by introductions of Continental roe, which are lighter in the coat. It is believed that some Perthshire roe were taken to Milton Abbas in Dorset in 1880.

The roe is a woodland species. It lies up in dense cover and feeds mainly at dawn and dusk. If there is no direct disturbance by man—such as in Rothiemurchus—roe can be almost confiding. There are districts in the Highlands where this dainty deer can be found on open hillsides, and where during the day it lies up in the cover of heather.

I prefer to watch roe with a background of woodland. My last sighting had been in the Black Wood of Rannoch, where I had disturbed a browsing buck. The animal froze, its greyness blending with the cathedral-like gloom between the tall trees. The deer turned and ran. I arrested its flight momentarily by giving a gruff bark. Moments later, now out of sight, the deer itself became vocal.

I could make a rough estimate of its rate of departure by hearing successive barks. It possibly passed near other deer, but no other barks were heard. I, in turn, must have walked near to roe, which do not bark unless they have become conscious of being seen. A deer that has escaped notice stands quite still—or silently sneaks away.

Rothiemurchus has an abundance of roe deer. Because the topography is varied, they can be seen—and sometimes heard—in all manner of situations. The ancestors of these roe were not slain with the savagery that occurred in some areas of central Scotland when the first ranks of young conifers were being planted. Any damage found was usually blamed on deer, whose population was promptly culled. Not only is there a more enlightened outlook by foresters but some thoughtful people believe that roe may have been wrongly blamed at times for what was really frost damage.

Roe deer are unsatisfactory beasts of the chase. Trained hounds were set against them in Glen More. When an animal was exhausted or cornered it was despatched by gunshot. Grigor

Grant was a celebrated stalker in Glen More, and he was not the first to be frustrated by roe.

Charles St John, of Morayshire, wrote that "the greatest drawback to preserving roe to any great extent is that they are so shy and nocturnal in their habits they seldom show themselves in daytime. I sometimes see a roe passing like a shadow through the trees, or standing gazing at me from a distance in some sequestered glade but, generally speaking, they are no ornament about the place, their presence being only known by the mischief they do to the young plantations and to the crops". He was referring to the roebuck's summertime habit of debarking saplings as it sets a scent. At this time, the undersides of branches might be scored.

Towards the end of the eighteenth century, Colonel Thornton, in these same Speyside forests, was introduced to Captain Grant, of Abernethy. The Colonel wanted a roebuck, and military precedence might have had something to do with the fact that Captain Grant put his foresters at the visitor's disposal.

"The day [of the hunt] was serene and charming for any purpose but deer-shooting. For the roebuck owes his preservation as much to his ears as his eyes; his organs of hearing are wonderfully acute, so that in a calm day . . . they are roused long before the shooter can get near them." The Colonel stumbled, twig-cracking and no doubt, cursing, all around Abernethy and saw only one roe. A shot was not made because the deer was far off. The sportsman concluded that stalking deer in the forest was "a very dangerous pursuit, by no means worth following".

The roe deer of Rothiemurchus fascinated Frank Wallace in a different way. He painted them, and possibly his best-known study is of a buck pursuing a coquettish doe, a picture titled *Unrequited Affection*. A roebuck becomes wild with excitement during the rut. Its pursuit of the doe is fierce, the copulation often savage, and if a rival turns up it is pugnaciously driven away.

On the following evening, I motored to Loch an Eilein and had a close view of a roebuck grazing a rocky hillside. My efforts at stalking were no less successful than the Colonel's had been.

At 80 yards the roe and I stared at each other, and then the deer was off for cover, displacing a few small stones in the process.

That roe was very little different in size and appearance from the roe after which the earliest human settlers went for some additional winter protein in their diet. There are slight weight variations in different areas—as with other deer—and the females are lighter than males, but the roe has been able to keep faithfully to the ancient mould.

Mr G. B. Macpherson-Grant shot roe deer at Ballindalloch, on lower Speyside, between 1889 and 1910. The weights of 18 bucks were noted by Frank Wallace, and the average gross weight was roughly 55 pounds. Mr Macpherson-Grant was plainly being selective in his shooting, taking the best of the stock, for an average weight for a Scottish roebuck is from about 40 to 60 pounds.

No roe were to be seen by Loch an Eilein until I had almost reached the derelict house called 'Mrs Cameron's Cottage'. To my left was the water, silvered where it caught the eye of the low-slung sun. Beyond the water, trees and hills. Trees were massed on one side of the cottage, but the front of the building overlooked some of the greenest grass I had seen in the Highlands. Here a doe grazed—and the beauty of the animal entranced me, as it had done the immortal Charles St John, though it did not stop him from slaying roe!

He explained, with an odd sense of values: "I never killed one without regretting it, and wishing that I could bring the poor animal back to life again. I do not think that roe are sufficiently appreciated as venison, between October and February, and of proper age. In summer, the meat is not worth cooking, being dry and sometimes rank." This last circumstance is due to the rut.

I had come to the Highlands at a time when the older roebuck, now in 'clean horn', were amorous. In most deer species, the rut comes in the autumn, but roe are typically individualistic. Spring is also the time when the master buck drives out all the younger bucks, and when a mature doe is heavy with a new season's crop of young.

As I watched the roe, some faint eddies of breeze must have carried the hated man scent to the deer, which became tense, looked briefly in my direction and, not stopping to confirm the original analysis of the situation, tripped off to the nearby wood. As I followed, the voices of disturbed roe preceded me. I understand from the experts that the voice of a buck is gruffer than that of a doe, and that it is possible to estimate the age of a beast by the relative deepness of the call. I doubt the latter point.

Where man does not disturb them, roe stay close to their home acres. Many are born, live and die in the same small tract of country. They do not herd like the more sociable red deer. In winter, if you see a party of roe, it will almost certainly be composed of a family—perhaps a buck, doe, kids and the young of the previous year. Such parties disperse early in the spring.

Roes are conspicuously individualistic. Most species of deer cast their antlers in spring. Yet in mid-March, when the Highland reds do this, the roebuck in the woodland has well-developed horn, having dropped the old pair of antlers in November. A roe doe with young kids will be mated by a buck in late July to August—a full two months before the rutting season of the red deer. The lovelorn buck gruntingly pursues a doe on a circular or figure-of-eight course which can often be seen clearly as a track around some natural feature, commonly a tree. 'Roe rings' are to be seen among the birches of Rothiemurchus.

The doe mated in early August carries a dormant seed until the end of the year, when it becomes implanted on the wall of the womb. The young, usually twins, are thus born at a time most favourable for young life—a period of good cover and nourishing food. Roe have been known to drop their calves in some odd places, even the centre of a road.

Man is the major predator, but there are other enemies. A golden eagle is able to lift the roe kid, and the wild cat will undoubtedly prey on young deer. A friend watched a roe kid being approached by a fox. The alarmed doe struck out with its forefeet in defence of its offspring. I heard a sad tale of a Highland wildlife park where a tame fox broke out from its enclosure and, before taking to the woods, slew a roe doe and its kid, which it cornered against wire netting.

I returned to the 'silage field' and counted eight roe, now just grey smudges in the gloom. How many cars had been parked during my absence while the occupants had a close view of the roe of Rothiemurchus? There must have been many. The animals, conditioned to the presence of traffic, ignored me totally!

12

RETURN OF THE REINDEER

They came pounding over the heather, broad feet raising jets of water from the patches of sphagnum—a dozen or more reindeer, third generation of Scottish reindeer, at home on the northern flanks of the Cairngorms, between the tree line and the diminishing drifts of snow.

The medium size of the reindeer did not disappoint me, as it had done a friend who expected much larger beasts. Not long before my Scottish jaunt I saw a television film shot in Siberia, where herders actually sit, well forward, on selected beasts. For its size—roughly three feet six inches at the withers—the reindeer must be immensely strong, though Siberian breeds are larger than those of Scandinavia, from which the present Scottish stock sprang.

On a rain-washed hillside in the Central Highlands I was surrounded by reindeer descended from a small experimental group loosed on Cairngorm slopes rich in 'reindeer moss', which is actually lichen. The experiment concerned the possibility of reindeer surviving and breeding in Scotland, and it was undertaken for a number of reasons. Reindeer could be another valuable source of tasty hill protein, and they do not compete with red deer at the grazings. Reindeer skin, hair and antler can be used for a variety of goods, useful, decorative or both. Additionally, the herd provides a fascinating subject for research. Every reindeer has a name, and its exact date of birth is usually known, with the result that no other deer herd in the world has yielded such comprehensive scientific records. Finally, the reindeer are undoubtedly attractive to the many tourists in the Glen More Forest Park.

It was in 1947 that a man had the idea of bringing reindeer to the Cairngorms, as I shall relate. The first animals arrived in 1952, and four years later the Department of Agriculture for Scotland recognized that the project had grown beyond the experimental stage. The research continues.

These Cairngorm reindeer ran directly towards me because I had a capacious camera bag. As I opened it, the animals thought they had detected a source of food. In fact, only a few reindeer are interested in tit-bits offered by visitors. Even while this small group nuzzled me, there were many other reindeer high on the range, in the bleak terrain of ptarmigan and blue hare. For many weeks of the year, no reindeer are enclosed and visitors must follow them into the corries and over the tops. The reindeer tend to stay on high ground in winter, for this is invariably drier.

When my camera case was seen to yield only a miscellany of metallic objects, the reindeer switched their attention to Mr Mikel Utsi, a reindeer-owner of Swedish origin, from Lapland, who brought the original stock to the Cairngorms. Mr Utsi has given the herd personal supervision for most of the intervening time. He opened a rucksack, which contained a small quantity of a supplementary mixture of cereals and beet—enough to keep a small number of reindeer on the lower land, where it could be easily seen.

Most of the reindeer, spread about their austere open grazings, must be viewed at random, from a distance. On the previous day, several women at the car park near the Cairn Gorm ski lift were pointing, with great excitement, at a group of three deer. For a prolonged view at close quarters I joined a conducted tour. With other people, I kept an appointment outside the stone-built Reindeer House, a home-cum-office for the keeper and for Mr Utsi, who is managing director of the Reindeer Company Ltd. This building is within easy reach of Loch Morlich. I eventually joined in a motorcade, following a van driven by Mr Utsi.

By the time we had parked our cars a thousand feet higher on the hill than our assembly point, the indecisive weather had made up its mind. It not only rained heavily but there was a gusty wind driving the rain at a 45-degree angle. Moorland which, on the previous day, had glowed invitingly in sunshine was now composed of a hundred murky tones. The sphagnum in the boggy places looked a bilious green.

We left our cars to take a pedestrian's route downwards, on a path that had been well pounded by the feet of visitors. Our legs were swished by ling and Mr Utsi, leading the way, used his thumbstick to flick away recently-deposited stones that might turn an ankle of a person wearing low shoes. His Karesuando Lapp headgear gave a festive air to the expedition—it was surmounted by a large red bobble!

Below us was a burn, thundering, frilly white with foam. We crossed a bridge and moved upwards on a gentle diagonal to a vast compound—and the group of reindeer kept near home largely for our benefit. I shivered as the first trickles of cold water coursed down my neck, and my top clothing soon bore the dark patches that signify total saturation by rain. The reindeer, in contrast, looked attentive and lively in their shelterless enclosure. If anything, the weather was not cold enough for them. The great advantage in keeping reindeer, says Mr Utsi, is that they find their own basic food, even under snow, and require no shelter.

A reindeer's thick winter coat was moulting away in unsightly tufts. This animal is darker in summer than in winter, when the off-white coat is given extra distinction by a silver mane. Now, in spring, new antlers had sprouted on the heads of the males. New horn grew lustily, cosseted by dark velvet.

I saw mineral licks, and some cast horn which had been chewed by animals feeling the need for extra calcium, as do the red deer. Mr Utsi had adorned what he considered to be the most tractable beasts with bells on cords, observing that other reindeer tend to congregate round the animals carrying bells. I clearly recall the pleasant jangling of bells as the reindeer moved around us. On that day there was little sound beyond the pattering rain.

Reindeer bull in late May, its growing antlers swathed in velvet
Reindeer cow, with moult-tattered coat, suckling its young

Caledonian pine forest almost in the shadow of the Cairngorms, near Derry Lodge

Tourists' Speyside: the path leads to an observation hut from where the Garten ospreys can be watched

A bull deer snuffled in my camera bag and, disappointed at the nature of the contents, turned away to graze. The burgeoning antlers were only a foot or two from where I stood. Mr Utsi explained that both sexes carry antlers, those of the bull reindeer being the larger. Bulls cast their headgear in late autumn, but horn-shedding by the cows—which carry small horns—is a springtime occurrence. It had happened a few weeks before my arrival. Antlers carried by the cow are indeed of value in repelling enemies of the calves dropped in spring, but even without them a cow reindeer can display aggression in the protection of its offspring, using the strength and power of the forefeet.

As I stood chatting with Mr Utsi, one of the enemies of young deer flew by. It was a hooded crow, maybe on some urgent mission concerning carrion. Another enemy is the fox. Free-ranging dogs threaten the herd, and during one year the calving season was ruined when vagrant dogs panicked the cows.

Mr Utsi, with the help of both paid and volunteer staff, delights a large number of holidaymakers by taking them to a type of deer normally found much further north than Britain. His enterprise has incidentally restored to the Highlands a species lost during the twelfth century.

Reindeer browsed on the tundral lands when the ice sheet relinquished its million-year-long hold on what is now Britain. There must have been quite large numbers of reindeer spread across the bleak lands in summer and wintering among trees. At the open grazings they would dine on lichen and dwarf birch, forerunner of the major birch and pine forests.

Ritchie, in The Influence of Man on Animal Life in Scotland, suggested that the ancient Scottish reindeer was a woodland variety as opposed to the "barren-ground" race, and that its decline was connected with the decline of the woods. He added:

Neolithic man had little influence on the forest, and the reindeer outlived him; but the Bronze and Iron Ages, with their demand for fuel for smelting, began a devastation which each succeeding age intensified, so that in the twelfth century, when Scottish laws were already endeavouring to conserve the forest, the last reference occurs to living reindeer in Scotland.

I

Another factor in the decline of the reindeer stocks would be the warming-up of the climate. The reindeer would probably move north until they came up against the sea. Here, in Caithness, the few survivors were haunted by the Jarls of Orkney, Rognvald and Harald, exploits described in the Orkneyinga saga.

Much earlier, man used a cave in Sutherland and here accumulated the remains of several hundred reindeer—a cache found earlier this century. It was in Caithness in 1816 that Robert Traill attempted to reintroduce the reindeer into Britain. He had a bull and two cows shipped from Archangel, but the last of them had died by the following spring. There were obviously too few animals to form a viable breeding nucleus. The reasons expressed at the time were "from want, it was believed, of their proper food, in addition to the supposed unsuitability of the climate".

For a brief period about 1820 there were reindeer on the southern foothills of the Cairngorms, in which area a small number was released by the Earl of Fife in the Forest of Mar, Aberdeenshire. Was this also a case of too few animals? Or did the Earl have the right idea but select the wrong type of reindeer? According to Scrope, the author of a book on Highland stalking, "they all died, not withstanding one of them was turned out on the summits, which are covered with dry moss, on which, it was supposed, they would be able to subsist". During the eighteenth century, fourteen reindeer brought to Dunkeld by the Duke of Atholl, and released on the Atholl Forest, did not survive long, dying off within two years.

Mr Utsi personally, and at his own expense, brought animals from his Swedish herd and later from southern Norway to the Central Highlands of Scotland. He included representatives of first mountain and then forest reindeer. The grand idea was developed one snowy afternoon in the spring of 1947 as he stood on the railway bridge at Aviemore. He had an outstanding view on the northern side of the Cairngorm range, and diagnosed "reindeer country", with which he had been familiar from his youth.

His family had owned reindeer for generations and was

descended from a people who had herded reindeer for a millennium. He had watched reindeer calves being born in May, and had taken part in the migration of the reindeer and their keepers, a movement beginning in May or June, from the highlands to the Norwegian coast. Here men and deer lived until September. The return journey was interrupted for a while at a half-way point so that the rituals of the rut could be enacted. The long round trip was completed in late December.

Mr Utsi brought reindeer to Scotland after a varied career which included catering, military service and the rescue of wartime refugees. The nucleus of the Cairngorm herd was moved over a thousand miles—by road, rail and sea—its leader being an old gelded male, Sarek, born on the slopes of Mount Sarek in northern Sweden. The eight reindeer of the first consignment arrived at Rothesay Dock aboard ss *Sarek*. The leader held its position in the herd for twelve years.

It was in Maytime that the first reindeer of modern times strode across the Highlands. At first, however, they were confined to 300 acres that had been made available by Colonel J. P. Grant, of Rothiemurchus. Wider and higher pastures were made available through the co-operation of the Forestry Commission, and on land recently acquired by the Highlands and Islands Development Board.

The establishment of the deer was not without worry. In the early days they suffered torment from flies, the summertime pests of many Highland mammals. Several animals were lost after fly-strike on a few hot summer days, but a special type of insect repellant was developed, and used during 1955. The liquid is sprayed on to the animals. The first reindeer calves to survive were born in 1955, and since then the herd has steadily increased. It numbered 92 beasts in 1971.

Mr Utsi has an easy familiarity with the reindeer. He makes no sudden movements and speaks to them as individuals, using their names. The Glen More reindeer are controlled by familiar voices, not by dogs as in Lapland. Sometimes Mr Utsi summons them by tooting on a horn. He is an expert with the lasso, as members of visiting societies have discovered when they have prevailed on him to give a demonstration. Mr Utsi has even lassoed a bull reindeer in the rut, when the otherwise docile animals can be aggressive.

The reindeer settled down in our presence. I watched them grazing, tearing at the coarse vegetation of the moor. A dark-coated calf of the year was being suckled by a cow while she fed on lichen.

It was interesting to hear of one way in which Mr Utsi quenches his thirst when out on the hills. He invariably carries the hollowed thigh bone of a Norwegian snow goose, using the bone as a straw for drinking from a moorland burn.

Now, soaked by rain, our little party made a brisk return to the cars. The reindeer, spread out across the moor, scorn shelter of any kind. They do not even seek cover in the woods.

13

OSPREYS AT GARTEN

Early in April—when, in Scotland, the first of the returning ospreys was planing down to alight on a veteran pine beside Loch Garten, at the edge of Abernethy Forest—I watched a young osprey at a reservoir five miles from my Pennine home. The bird lingered here for over a week. Its leisurely flight northwards with the spring might end in Scotland or be extended to Scandinavia.

This osprey ignored the pole surmounted by a cartwheel that had been set up in the hope a pair of vagrant birds would stay and nest. I watched its distinctive, even spectacular, method of fishing, during which it plucks fish from just under the surface of the water.

The 'fish hawk' hovered, lined itself up on a fish, half closed its wings and descended to strike the water feet first. For a few moments it was enveloped in spray, and water dripped from its feathers as it fought its way into the air again, the fish so arranged that it met the air head on, reducing drag.

It has been known for osprey to fix their needle-sharp claws into really large fish and to be dragged under water during the ensuing struggle. Generally, a bird selects a fish weighing a pound or two—a size it is capable of controlling. In the Highlands there is a strong preference for pike. The claws close on a fish like a vice. Scaly underparts to the osprey's feet further enable it to retain its grasp on a slippery, wriggling prey.

I had been in Scotland for only half a day when I again saw

an osprey in flight, this time at the Loch of Lowes, near Dunkeld, where a pair of osprey nested successfully for the first time in 1971. In the previous season, a gale blew nest and eggs from the chosen tree. As the 'fish hawk' swept by I saw features of its distinctive plumage: deep brown above, white beneath; white head, a band of brown extending through the eye to the nape; and dusky band on the breast. A small crest on the head can be seen when the big bird is in repose.

It was early evening. I recall the yaffle of a green woodpecker and, in the grey dusk, a family party of roe deer wandering along the edge of the loch. The osprey nests in much wilder Highland country than this, but wherever it settles there are certain basic requirements—woodland and fresh water, little populated and unpolluted by man.

My third encounter with the osprey that spring was in the Spey valley, but before I watched the famous Loch Garten pair I listened to the owner of a guest house as he described, in matter-of-fact tones, with no trace of excitement in his voice, how an osprey had recently descended to the lochan just behind the house and had lifted from the water what appeared to be small pike. Had this particular bird come from Garten, or from another, as yet undisclosed, nesting site in the Central Highlands?

The return of the ospreys to Garten is, even more than the first calling of the cuckoo, a keenly-awaited interlude of the Highland spring. A roadman I met near Boat of Garten explained the feeling of anticipation as being similar to that when a member of the family is due back from a long holiday. "I don't seem to be able to concentrate on anything for a week or two before the birds turn up again."

Unlike the golden eagles, which are virtually sedentary, simply consigning the young of the year into the outer world without even a kind word, the buzzard-sized osprey travels to its nesting area from afar. Wings with a span of about four and a half feet carry a bird from its wintering grounds to the south of Europe. In its northward progression the bird stops at freshwater lakes and reservoirs to feed, preen and rest.

A number of ospreys seen in Britain will nest in Scandinavia, Swedish birds (like those in the Highlands) showing a partiality for pines as nesting sites. Presumably, the ospreys of Scotland are from Scandinavian stock. The re-colonization of the Highlands began in the early 1950s and has continued so successfully that now at least seven pairs breed regularly.

Loch Garten is ringed by pines. The most an ordinary visitor to the observation hut will see is the gleam of water in the middle distance, for the hut was deliberately set well back from the shore. So there is an air of mystery about Garten—mystery that is intensified when someone relates the story of a local spectre, *glaistig*, an old man with foreknowledge of the deaths of members of the house of Gartenmore. The *glaistig* bellowed out whenever a death was imminent; he presumably worked himself out of a job with the demise of the last member of the family.

The road from Aviemore to Garten was well marked, as befits its importance, for now it is followed by close on 40,000 eager osprey-hunters a year. The birds have become a symbol of man's need to preserve and encourage the remnants of a declining avifauna. They also symbolize one way in which the economy of a very rural area can benefit from creatures that become a major tourist attraction. Every other house in the district was offering bed-and-breakfast.

The name Boat of Garten intrigued me. It relates to a ferry that became redundant in 1899, when the river bridge was constructed. I parked my car near Loch Mallachie, 'loch of the curse', where—'tis said—a young woman crossing a burn to meet her lover on the morning of their wedding day was drowned; the demented lover cursed the place.

There is a curse on Garten, too. It is the Egg-Collector. The rarer a bird becomes, the greater is the value of its eggs, and in the case of an osprey they are most beautifully coloured eggs: cream, boldly blotched and spotted with reddish brown and chocolate. Stolen eggs are swaddled in cotton wool and gloated over in secret by a few eccentric people.

The RSPB does its best to protect the Garten birds. Raiders come up against barbed wire, electrical warnings, sensitive micro-

phones and volunteer wardens. Many attempts at larceny must
have been thwarted, but some raids succeed. It was the disappearance of the eggs in 1958 that led to round-the-clock
wardening. A fortnight before my visit someone had entered the
area shortly after midnight on a moonless night, scaled the tree
and departed with the eggs. The electrical gadgetry had been
giving trouble at the time. The wardens knew nothing of the
raid until they heard, in the darkness, the wild screams of the
outraged and terrified ospreys.

Such alarm calls have echoed down the years. In the Victorian
age 'sportsmen' also shot the adult birds. Anglers, lacking a real
insight into the osprey's food preferences, presumed them guilty
of competing for the most desirable fish and cheered whenever
a bird was destroyed.

The most savage campaigns against ospreys were undertaken
by Charles St John, for he concentrated on this species. He
described some of his activities in A Tour of Sutherland, mirror-
ing a strange blend of emotions—joy in the beauty of the osprey,
"a picturesque bird"; assertions that it harmed no-one's interests;
and elation at having destroyed it. "Why the poor osprey should
be persecuted I know not," he wrote, "as it is quite harmless,
living wholly on fish, of which everyone knows there is too
great an abundance in this country for the most rigid preserver
to grudge this bird his share."

Visiting a nest near Scourie, he shot a hen osprey and took
two eggs from the nest. Later, at Rhiconich, he tried unsuccessfully to shoot a bird while his companion, Dunbar, swam across
a loch to its island nest and returned with a half-grown young
bird and an addled egg. At a third nesting site, St John shot
the male and Dunbar took three young birds from the nest. The
men, always thorough, then returned to Scourie, where the male
osprey was found to have acquired another mate. The men took
two eggs from the eyrie.

Colonel Thornton saw ospreys during his Highland jaunt in
the eighteenth century, recording that

> we landed at the romantic Inchmerin (an island in Loch
> Lomond). . . . We had, in the course of the day, seen an *offrey*,

or water-eagle, make some noble dashes into the lake after her prey, and understanding from one of the boatmen that there was an *eyrie* on a small island, in our voyage home I ordered them to attempt to get as near the nest as possible, and loaded my gun well, wishing to kill her as a specimen.

Notwithstanding all our precaution, however, she rose long before we got near the island; at least we perceived a bird of some kind, for it was too dark to distinguish of what sort, at the distance we lay. These birds are very rare; in all my different excursions, I never heard of any except at Loch Lomond and Loch Morlaix, in Glenmore.

His last reference was presumably to Loch Morlich.

The last pair of ospreys to inhabit the area of Loch Lomond were killed by John Colquhoun in the middle of the nineteenth century. He shot the female, trapped the male but—like Charles St John—could become lyrical about the species.

They were a beautiful pair—the female, as in most birds of prey, being considerably the larger. The eggs of these ospreys had been taken every year, and yet they never forsook their eyrie. It was a beautiful sight to see them sail into our bay on a calm summer night, and after flying round it several times, strike down a good-sized pike, and bear it away as if it had been a minnow.

Osprey nested on the ruined castle of Loch an Eilein, where they received protection from the Grants of Rothiemurchus. The estate's boat was kept padlocked during the nesting season and the men were posted to keep watch on the nest. Yet when the collectors provided a monetary stimulus, brave men (and, whatever their other shortcomings, they were brave) risked death by drowning as they swam in the icy loch by night.

Elizabeth Grant, in her *Memoirs of a Highland Lady*, published in 1808, was content to watch the ospreys. "Often the birds rose . . . and wheeled, skimming over the loch in search of the bird required by the young eaglets, who could be seen peeping over the pile of sticks that formed their home."

The main thief at Loch an Eilein went by night. He tied one end of a rope round his waist—a precaution against being afflicted by cramp—and handed the other end of the rope to his companion. He then swam naked to the island. Climbing on to the castle, he took the eggs, and then found he had a major problem, that of transporting the eggs to the mainland. He had no clothes, and therefore no pockets! The thief clutched an egg in each hand, lay on his back in the water and was drawn rapidly across. The raid was successfully repeated in the following year.

The last reliable date for ospreys nesting in Scotland—until the species' triumphant return in recent times—is believed to be 1908 at Loch Arkaig, Inverness-shire, though ospreys may have bred at Loch Loyne, in the same country, until 1916. Loch Arkaig was visited by Richard and Cherry Kearton, the latter of whom pioneered bird photography in Britain, in 1899. It was a scorching hot day in a droughty summer, only fourteen years before the last osprey was seen wheeling around this loch.

Richard reported: "While my brother was preparing to make a study of the eyrie, and its builders perched on the dead tree tops of an adjoining island, the female, as if afraid the hot sunshine would do harm to her exposed eggs, plunged headlong into the loch and, rising, shook her dripping wings over them, after which she quietly resumed her favourite perch". It was noticed that a pair of starlings had reared their young in a nest among sticks forming the eyrie.

The osprey did not entirely desert Scotland. Passage migrants were occasionally seen using a western approach to their Scandinavian nesting haunts. The first Scottish nest of modern times was found in 1955, and four years later a pair raised its young at Loch Garten. I went here thankful that by managing 677 acres as a bird reserve, the RSPB had been able to report a number of cases of ospreys nesting and rearing their young to independence. This cordon of concern also benefits other bird species, and watchers have seen a Slavonian grebe on the loch.

If there had been no signs near Garten I would not have hesitated on my way to the observation hut. I saw a score of parked cars. No longer do parts of the approach path flood, for a 'peat road' was made, again by volunteer labour. As I strode into the gloomy area between pines, a chaffinch 'pinked' and I observed the coal tit.

The views opened out. On either side of the track lay heather, blaeberry, some cranberry, exposed tree roots and a sprinkling of medium-sized pine and scrub oak. The peat was dark and rich, like chocolate cake. From it grew tufts of a great peat-forming plant, the so-called cotton-grass, which is actually a sedge. I was told of the family parties of crossbills seen in this area about June, and of the crested tits which have been found nesting not far from the observation hut.

A warden spoke mainly of the osprey—of raiders foiled and raiders who got through. A man who stole the eggs dropped them and they were broken. A vandal almost sawed through the nesting tree, which had to be reinforced by strips of iron. The osprey nest had also suffered from gales, which in 1963 actually blew the female and her eggs from the nest.

There was an air of gloom about the little company assembled in the observation hut, queueing to view the ospreys through powerful binoculars trained on the birds. I should have been able to see the spectacle of an osprey arriving with food for the young, throwing its wings so well forward they obscured its vision of all but the nest ahead, and setting the tail at a downward angle to assist with the braking process, while a big fish held in a vice-like grip glistened as it caught the eye of the sun.

The warden, a young man from London who was spending part of his holiday supervising the osprey, told me the sequel to the sad chronicle of the nest raided and eggs stolen. The birds built a 'frustration eyrie'. In a previous year the site for such an eyrie was novel, to say the least—the monument erected near Aviemore to a Duke of Gordon!

One of two pairs of binoculars in the observation hut was trained on the disconsolate ospreys which had alighted on a distant tree and were so immobile they could have been stuffed birds set up to console visitors. This cynical thought vanished when the male shuffled its narrow wings and left them hanging loosely. That was all! I trudged back along the 'peat road', cursing all egg-collectors.

Normally these Garten birds remain in the vicinity of the eyrie until the end of August, sometimes early September, and then drift southwards—across Britain and over continental Europe to wintering grounds that contrast vividly with the Highlands in which the birds were reared.

In 1972 the ospreys of Garten nested successfully.

14

FLAME-EYED EAGLE

Twice, during that Highland spring, the lordly form of a golden eagle passed before me. On each occasion the sighting was unexpected. I had not intended to look for eagles and had no knowledge of an eyrie's location, being content to know that an appreciable number are used each year.

Pantingly, I breasted a high ridge, and an eagle rose up. I saw an immense bird clad in dark brown feathers, yellowish about the head and neck. The eagle moved with slow, shallow wing beats, questing for an updraught on a day when there was little detectable movement of the air. Beyond the rim of the hill, the wings were held stiffly outwards, the tips of the primaries extending like dark fingers, curving upwards at the ends.

Now the eagle was simply using the power of rising air, being pushed aloft by pressure under broad wings that would be about six feet in span, and with tail moving subtly. The course taken by the bird was steep and straight. There was not a sound to signify movement. I watched, fascinated, as the eagle was dwarfed by distance—until it was little more than a dot, a minute blemish, on the underside of a grey cloud high above.

The second eagle—and it really was another bird—appeared as I rested in a small glen, my back couched by springy heather. This bird circled almost above me. Having been accustomed to seeing buzzards, which are not true eagles, I had the wrong sense of scale.

What appeared to be a starling rose from some crags to harry the hawk. When the intruder gave voice, I was astonished to hear the call of a crow, presumably a hooded crow. Identification was difficult because the bird flew against the brightness of the sky and was in silhouette. So, too, was the eagle. The Gaelic name, *iolaire dubh*, meaning 'black eagle', is surely an allusion to the bird seen in these circumstances.

The eagle turned eastwards, beating its broad wings infrequently, to compensate for the absence of strong air currents. In its wide circling, several miles away, the eagle was partly moving in cloud and partly in the open sky.

William Wordsworth called the eagle "flame-eyed". He was a young man in the English Lake District at a time when the last members of the eagle tribe were attempting to nest there. The very last pair, of white-tailed eagles, hopefully laid a clutch of eggs in Eskdale during the 1780s. Wordsworth and his sister, Dorothy, may have seen eagles during their Highland journey.

"Flame-eyed" is a good term, but watchers at the Highland eyries find that if they make the slightest movement they come under a clear, icy gaze. Wordsworth should not be taken literally. It is the spirit of his words that matters!

The golden eagle is a glamour bird in the Highlands and might have been made for romance. Huge, regal in appearance, frequenting the vast barrenlands to which man's persecution has banished it—but having returned to nest in Ireland and England —the eagle survives in an age which favours smaller, less conspicuous creatures.

I hasten to add that eagles do not normally flaunt themselves before the human gaze. They are shy in the presence of people, and comparatively few visitors have good close views of them. Many visitors would not recognize an eagle if they saw one outside a zoo, where an approach to a distance of a few feet is possible.

A golden eagle can easily lose itself in the vastness of a deer forest, the type of country which has been its salvation, given enlightened estate management. It is estimated that each pair of golden eagles needs about 10,000 acres of deer forest to sustain it. The eyrie of an eagle, a big twiggy jumble, set on a ledge—though more frequently on Scots pine in the region of the Caledonian Forest—may be prominent to those with eyes to see, but when an eagle is at rest away from the nest the bird can be infuriatingly inconspicuous, leaving just a few droppings and the odd cast feather as visiting cards. One of the advantages an eagle has over many other birds is the ability to conserve its energy and to fast for long periods when food is scarce.

The golden eagle is frequently an eater of carrion, and one or two naturalists have had the unkindly thought of comparing it with the vulture. An eagle has been seen staggering away from a feast of sheep or deer in a heavy, ungainly fashion, scarcely able to take flight. Yet this monarch of the sky is capable of superb diving, after which it will clasp live prey—a blue hare, a bird, a fox cub or even a deer calf—with an unyielding grip.

The eagle can reputedly 'stoop' with the speed of a peregrine falcon, but more often it moves low down, beating into the wind, almost brushing the ground, panicking into flight a normally close-sitting ptarmigan, or startling a recumbent blue hare into incautious movement. The eagle invites them to run —and die.

My sighting of eagles, in an area well off the main roads, came when I had lost faith in the possibility of such an encounter. I looked for eagles, of course. My eyes prickled as I stared skywards for long periods. Every other man I met in the remote places (and there were not many people here) had seen an eagle the day before! Observing an eagle is possible for those with the time and energy to trudge in eagle country. Highland eagles are mainly sedentary. After the nesting season, the young move out. Having gained independence, they must find terri-tories of their own, and the wind carries very inexperienced birds into new areas where, quite often in the past, they were shot or trapped. Game interests were paramount, and game-keepers accused eagles of the wholesale disturbance of game birds. Or there were shepherds ready to condemn the eagles, however wrongly, for stealing young lambs. Fifteen golden eagles figured in a list of 'vermin' destroyed at an estate by the Garry between 1837 and 1840.

Happily for the status of the golden eagle in Scotland, the deer forests remained to provide seclusion and food for the main stock. They were also 'reservoirs' from which adjacent districts could be regularly replenished. It is to the advantage of the golden eagle that it has a long breeding life once maturity has been reached, at the age of three or four years. An old Gaelic saying makes the point of an eagle's longevity with some understandable exaggeration: "Thrice the age of a dog the age of a horse; thrice the age of a horse the age of man; thrice the age of a man the age of a stag; thrice the age of a stag the age of an eagle; thrice the age of an eagle the age of an oak tree".

The antagonism of countryfolk led to the extinction of the golden eagle in England towards the end of the eighteenth century. The Reverend H. A. Macpherson, who wrote extensively about the fauna of the Lake District, recorded that "a long and strong rope was kept in Borrowdale, by subscription, for the purpose of letting down men into the rocks to take the nests and young of Eagles. . . ." One man was drawn up in fear and trembling, two or three strands of the rope having been badly chafed by the sharp edges of the rocks.

The late Ernest Blezard told me the story of the shooting of a vagrant eagle in Dunnerdale about 1860. Farmer Jenkinson carried a muzzle-loader with him on his rounds and he managed one or two unsuccessful shots at the eagle. The farmer then decided to stay concealed at one place and, ramming a "turrible gurt charge" of powder and lead down his weapon, he lay flat on his back in the heather.

The eagle sailed overhead. Farmer Jenkinson fired vertically, winged the bird—and himself sustained a broken collarbone from the violence of the gun's recoil. The eagle fell into a dam and "gave further account of itself before it was despatched and carried home . . . where its full-spread wings were found almost to span the small kitchen".

The eagle has returned to the Lake District, with the southward spread of Scottish birds. For some years before the first

Flame-eyed eagle. A golden eagle at its Highland eyrie

Two eaglets, now well-feathered, at the eyrie

English nest in about two centuries was found, an eyrie was occupied just north of Solway Firth. Soaring above the blue hills of southern Scotland, the birds would be able to look beyond the shimmering firth to the dark hills of Cumbria.

There were certain prescribed ways of killing Highland eagles. One of them was the use of a metal trap baited with dead lambs. Eventually the eagle received legal—if not actual—protection. The latest menace to Highland birds came quietly, insidiously. Eagles gorging themselves on the carcasses of sheep which had died from some of the weird complaints that afflict these animals, took in a quantity of dieldrin, a toxic ingredient of sheep dip. When dieldrin had built up in the eagles' bodies to a sufficient strength, it led to infertility in the birds. During the 1960s, naturalists were reporting the failure of many pairs to hatch out their eggs, the shells of which were seen to be noticeably thinner than normal. When dieldrin was banned, a slow recovery of the species became possible.

Sportsmen who trained dashing birds like the peregrine falcon to fly at prey were always disappointed that they could not make good use of the golden eagle. When Colonel Thornton sojourned in Badenoch, a Highlander offered him an eagle, suggesting that the bird might be broken in and used against game. But, noted the Colonel, "they cannot be made any use of, from their immense weight, and from the shape of their wings".

Eagles "can have no speed, except when at their place; then, to be sure, their weight increases their velocity, and they certainly aim with an incredible swiftness, like a cannonball, seldom missing their quarry". From their "unwieldy make and prodigious appetite, they are inconvenient, expensive birds in a menagerie".

A Highlander he met had a cunning ruse in order to obtain food for his family. He took an eaglet,

and by tethering it, and watching the old ones, which regularly came to feed it, and taking away such provisions as they bring, which consist of fauns of the roe, lambs, kids, hares, black game, grouse, or ptarmigants, wild-ducks, &c, he amply supplies his

K

family for some weeks; consequently it is a great acquisition to him.

Writers in the Wordsworth mould have pictured the golden eagle as a regal bird. It looks regal when it is seen soaring high or perched on a tree sprouting from a crag. Other writers, as already noted, have pointed to its affinities with the vulture—especially its love of gorging itself on gobbets of flesh from dead sheep or the grallochs of red deer slain during the stalking season. Sheep are not common in the Central Highlands, where eagles turn to other fare, mainly red grouse. They flush and fly down ptarmigan, have been known to slay other birds—among them crows and pigeons—and lift young mammals back to their eyries. Eaglets pick up red deer calfs and fox cubs. In the Lake District an eagle dived on, and carried for a little way, a small terrier which had been romping ahead of its owner, a gamekeeper. Outside the nesting season, golden eagles have been seen to strike at migrating grey geese.

I have already commented on the eagle's ability to fast in lean times. This advantage is not universal. When a hard winter is ending the golden eagle may regularly fill itself with flesh torn from the corpses of creatures starved to death.

An appreciable number of Highland eagles do not live up to the popular conception, which is of a bird residing in remote, barren countryside, its nesting site being on an inaccessible ledge. I heard of tree-nesting eagles during my jaunt to the west of Pitlochry. Now, in Speyside, there were further stories of birds that select trees, usually Scots pine, high up the slopes, away from the main tourist routes. Enough material to fill a small cart might be piled on the tree's branches to create a nesting platform, the nesting cavity itself being lined with softer material, often the great wood rush. Most of the Highland eyries are situated between the 1,000 and 2,000 feet contour lines, but generalization can be deceptive. One pair of eagles may have two, even three eyries. It has been known for such a pair to nest on a cliff site one year and on a tree during the following season.

There is a winter chill on the landscape when eagles start

their nesting programme. Birds have been seen carrying nesting material in January. A well-used eyrie is patched, augmented and, during the nesting season, adorned with fresh foliage— rowan, juniper, even tufts of heather.

The number of eggs laid is commonly two, but an aged female may produce only one. In lean years two eaglets may hatch out but only one survive. Golden eagles, like owls, begin to incubate with the laying of the first egg, which leads to a disparity of age between the eaglets. The elder, having the advantage of age, may prevent its young brother or sister from acquiring enough to eat and will also tend to bully the younger bird.

For about a third of the year, the eyrie is the focal point of an eagle's life. Incubation begins towards the end of March, and over 40 days elapse before the eggs hatch. The birds, struggling from the shells, soon dry off and are seen to be clad in soft, downy white, an insulation against the extremities of the weather. For about six weeks the young have their food presented to them. The male bird provides it, and the female tears it up and offers it daintily. Then the prey is dumped at the eyrie; the young must tear it up for themselves.

Highland eagles are strangely silent birds. One of the men who makes a regular round of eyries at Whitsuntide to attach rings to the legs of eaglets (a check can then be made on their future movements) reports that over many years he has rarely heard an eagle calling. He was therefore startled in a recent year when, handling an eaglet, he heard it give a moderately loud scream. Usually, when disturbed, the incubating adult flies off silently, pitches down at a favourite perch maybe two miles away, and waits patiently for the intruder to leave.

This large species has not only maintained a reasonable population in the Highlands but has sent its emissaries into Ireland and England. Wordsworth, who referred to the "flame-eyed" eagle, would have been delighted if he could have foreseen that eagles would return to the Lake District. Today a pair nests not many miles from the poet's old home at Grasmere.

15

ON THE ACHLEAN TRAIL

"Glen Feshie? Turn left, just before Feshie Bridge. If you find yourself going downhill, then you've gone too far!" The farmer spoke in perfectly good English. There was none of the extreme provincialism one is led to expect by reading books about the Highlands—just a Scottish intonation to add character to the words.

I asked him about the hairy trout that were supposed to live in Lochan Gael, near where the Feshie pours its whisky-brown water into the Spey. He ignored the question. Neither did he respond to my reminder that Glen Feshie is supposed to be haunted by fairies.

Naturally, having lived in these parts for some years, he had heard the story of the local laird who, believing that his young and beautiful wife was a witch, tried to drown her in the river. As she was being swept away, the laird changed his mind, jumped into the Feshie and saved her life.

Glen Feshie is in wild Badenoch, and the name means 'wet glen'. I found it hard to judge whether lower Feshie is wet or dry, for the Forestry Commission has set down a dense mass of conifers. At the moment, many of them are young—just a green stubble on the floor of the glen. Conifers extend in dark and uniform ranks almost to Achlean, beyond which stands one of the celebrated 'black woods' composed of Scots pine. After an interlude of open country, where the ground is generally very wet, more pines are seen. There are birches, too. Both testify to nature's ability to clothe the green skin of the earth with trees. They also indicate the extent of the old Caledonian Forest, being a last great flourish of pines along the edge of the Cairngorms.

Where open country remains in Glen Feshie, the curlew dips and calls. Ring-ouzels fly, chacking, down the gorges. The thin whistle of the golden plover punctuates the spring days on the high land. Walk on the hill slopes, and you will have your legs whipped by heather.

Feshie's neighbour, to the west, is Glen Tromie, extending to the wilds of Gaick. At about 1,500 feet in Gaick is a remote, solitary lodge, and not far from it lie three lochs seen by only the most energetic of travellers. The finest of them, Loch Duin, lies in a wedge between hills strewn by small rocks in the form of fan-shaped screes. It always reminds me of Wastwater, in the Lake District.

When I think of Feshie I think initially of trees—Christmas trees that give the planter a moderately quick cash crop. The presence of the Forestry Commission has brought advantages to life in the Highlands. Jobs have been provided for men in the Feshie area, where the Commission's largest forestry project in Strathspey is being developed. Over 6,000 acres will ultimately be afforested at Inshriach, near the foot of Glen Feshie. Young forests teem with voles and attract predators such as short-eared owls and kestrels. Eventually the trees blot out the light from the ground, which contains a sterilizing mat of dead leaves. Birds like goldcrests and titmice benefit from afforestation, and in due course even the capercaillie may be interested. This bird usually congregates where pines are at least 20 feet high.

Another blessing, this time for tourists in a hurry, is the Forestry Commission's improvement of the old track east of the Feshie as far as Achlean. The major route west of the water was mainly intended to give quick transit to the Lodge—a sporting establishment set among pines and birches, beyond which the tracks are indicated on maps by means of broken rules; they are of doubtful quality.

Once they were for men on foot, or for the riders of horses. Along them were led stocky ponies carrying slain deer to the

Lodge, for Feshie has long been a sporting estate, being originally
owned by the Dukes of Gordon. The ubiquitous Land Rover now
leaves tyre marks—visiting cards deep-printed in long strips—
where once a man would be considered mad to take a motor
vehicle.

Glen Feshie is, to all intents and purposes, a cul-de-sac, but
walkers can trudge on to Braemar, in the valley of the Dee, as
part of a 28-mile journey from Kincraig. They climb to 1,834
feet at the watershed. For centuries men have dreamed about a
road that would connect the two valleys. John Taylor, writer of
the *Pennyless Pilgrimage* (1618) may have longed for some form
of surfaced road when he strode from Braemar to "Ruthen" in
"Bagenoch". General Wade dreamed of such a road, and even
sent his engineer to look into the possibilities. Nothing came of
the idea, nor of the subsequent request made by Queen Victoria
that a road should be considered, nor of the scheme, of much
more recent origin, by the Ministry of Transport.

Glen Feshie remains wild, grand, remote. Because it is broad,
and lies at about 1,500 feet above sea level, it is essentially moorland in character. And there is an awesome backdrop in the
massif forming the most westerly flourish of the Cairngorms,
extending to over 3,500 feet above sea level. These craggy hills
are ponderous. They have the hunch-backed appearance imparted
by savage glaciation. Their Gaelic names are strange to Sassenach
ears. Prefaced by *creag*, which means rock, they include
Mhigeachaidh and Ghiubhsachan!

The sight of a field used by a gliding club made me scan the
sky, for where there are gliders there is usually a locale noted
for its thermals, and where thermals exist it is reasonable to
expect to see a golden eagle or, failing this, a buzzard. The only
bird in flight honked its identity—carrion or hooded crow.

To Glen Feshie, in less urgent times, came Sir Edwin Landseer,
darling artist of the Victorians—the man who achieved enduring
fame in the Highlands through his study of *The Monarch of the
Glen* which, incidentally, features the Cairngorms in the background. I cannot be certain that this painting was based on
studies made in Glen Feshie, but some of his other deer studies

undoubtedly were. They have sentimental Victorian titles—
Waiting for the Deer to Rise and *Stealing a March*. Landseer
also painted a fresco above the fireplace in a bothy that had
been erected when the Duchess of Bedford was lessee of the
forest. The huts were succeeded by a pretentious lodge in the
shadow of Carn Dearg.

The new-surfaced road to Achlean was like a thick dark crust
along the Wet Glen. My journey along it was rather dull, difficult to recall, for the sky held an unbroken mass of grey clouds
and the hills, lacking the lighting effects of direct sunlight, were
not inspiring. They showed up but faintly through mist.
I passed innumerable young conifer trees. After the first few
thousand had flashed by the car my mind no longer registered
trees clearly.

The road dipped into the yard of Achlean, a former farm lying
near the foot of Carn Ban Mor, its name meaning 'wide field'.
An oyster-catcher was probing the lawn with a tangerine bill.
The bird's pied plumage—even the delicate flesh-pink of the legs
—showed up well against the bright spring grass. I was mobbed
by farmyard fowls, one of which scrambled into the car when
I unwisely left the door open.

The clucking of hens sounded where, in times past, visitors
heard the bleating of many sheep, then—at a later period—the
lowing of cattle, dark Highland stock. Sometimes the lowing
was in concert, for one of the old drove roads passed through
Feshie, the cattle being driven to the tryst at Falkirk. Today,
the hens clucked with little competition. Clucking was virtually
the only sound I heard until a power saw being used by an
unseen forester working among conifers across the river broke
the afternoon calm with its wasp-like buzzing.

It attracted my attention to the western hill, now standing
waist-deep in spruce. It was a curious hill, horizontally marked,
almost as though it had been brought into being not by nature
but by a draughtsman sitting at a drawing board. Each mark
represented a terrace, and collectively the terraces showed the old
levels of the river plain. Ravens are said to nest on the crags;
I neither heard nor saw them. There was just the clucking of

the Achlean hens, and the trill of a sandpiper, and the zit, zit, zit of a departing dipper.

Achlean is at the heart of a nature trail which has borrowed the farm's name. The Nature Conservancy and the owner, Lord Dulverton, devised a two-mile walk, and it was the title that had originally drawn me to it. Achlean Trail! It would not be out of place in the Injun Country of Manitoba!

I strode on rising ground. At the pathside was a multitude of plants where, from a distance, I would have suspected that only heather grew. Here was cowberry, which is sometimes called Scots cranberry. The blaeberry seemed as much at home on these open hills as it had been in the pine woods of Strathspey. Bearberry was also reasonably plentiful. Somewhere on the tops grew the romantic cloudberry.

I could see almost half the trail from Achlean. A tawny line of beaten ground extended to the nearest horizon. Eventually the path breasted the ridge, dipped to a burn and headed purposefully for the topside of a pinewood, where a tower had been erected for those with the patience to look for red deer. Deer do not stand about, waiting to be photographed by visitors. They are masters of the art of losing themselves to human sight, even in an expanse of heather. I scanned the slopes for a quarter of an hour before I saw patches of rust-red against the dun-coloured wilderness. Here were hinds, half a dozen perhaps. Later, I saw a herd of over 30 deer on the skyline, a long way off. It was pointless to try and reach them directly.

Red deer, with astonishing adaptability, settled down to life on the bleak hills when man took over in the glens and toppled the trees. Scanning the broad vista of heathered slopes from the tower on the Achlean Trail I marvelled at the ability of a hind to drop a calf and rear it to the stage where it can follow briskly where there is virtually no cover. Yet it would be happening soon. A hind, feeling that the birth of its calf is imminent, will move a little away from the group, deliver the calf into a heathery bed, suckle it, nudge it down, and let it remain, immobile and inconspicuous, until it is strong enough to run at foot and the group of females can be rejoined.

Dotterel on the Cairngorms. The cock incubates the eggs and attends
to the chicks

On the Achlean Trail. The stream takes meltwater from snowfields on
the High Cairngorms

Red deer calf at a Highland wildlife park

Red hinds wintering in woodland: the sexes consort only during the rutting season

Red deer grazing at the edge of a stand of Scots pine

Feshie is dominantly a stag forest. The stags, I presumed, were higher up the hill slopes, still recuperating after the privations of winter, and keeping pace, through selective grazing, with the drain on their resources attending the growing of new antlers. High up on the hills it is cooler, drier, breezier than in the glens. Stags can thus escape the worst torments of the fly menace. Human visitors to the Highlands in summer tend to stay on low ground, and spend much time swatting a variety of winged insects! My 1927 edition of *Muirhead's Scotland* contains some advice to tourists about insect pests. Visitors should carry oil of citronella, or some similar preparation, against "the attacks of 'midges', which are very troublesome in the evenings, especially near water".

Into Glen Feshie came the sportsmen. There was Lord Henry Bentinck who, carrying a muzzle-loader, followed a 13-pointer for "two nights and a day". During that time he subsisted on "a few sandwiches left for lunch and a wee drop in the flask". Details of the expedition were jotted down by the Duke of Portland, who considered that "for sheer determination, hardiness and keenness the exploit is equalled only by Charles St John's chase of the 'Muckle Hart of Benmore' ".

Lord Henry eventually came close to the stag, which lay on a knoll. "It was now getting late, and as the beasts were only a short distance from the Atholl March, Lord Henry decided to chance a shot," noted the Duke of Portland. The stalker had a sudden doubt about the state of the charge in the gun. It had been prepared on the morning of the previous day, and there had been storms during the night. Was it still good—or damp and useless? Keeping calm, Lord Henry withdrew the charge and loaded afresh, "a delicate operation with hinds lying within a few yards". He shot the stag.

Sir Charles Mordaunt, leasing the forest between 1878 and 1891, used a rifle and at least twice he slew over 100 stags in a season. The tenant in 1893, Baron J. W. H. Schröder, bagged a stag which had a 13-point head. The span was measured at 24 inches inside and 38 inches outside.

The deer of Glen Feshie are not left entirely helpless in bleak mid-winter. They are prevented by fences from entering the new plantations, but they wander down among the pines of the small wood near Achlean. These trees shelter them and offer food in hard times, for the pines are attended by junipers which a hungry deer will browse. I saw several trees where red deer had rubbed themselves, possibly during the irritation of the spring moult. They did not appear to have rolled on the nests of black ants (as they do in north-west England), and the ants' main irritants were humans, who had pelted the nests with large stones.

Now I heard the roar of water—a burn creaming over grey rocks, close to pines before levelling out at the final approach to the Feshie. Melt-water from snowfields was mainly responsible for the spectacular series of cascades. Lower down, streams had been bridged by ghillies to provide crossing points for themselves and ponies bearing deer carcasses.

Over in Gaick, deer have been known to perish from avalanches racing down the steep slopes of treeless hills. From here, during the 1914–18 world war, ponies carried slain deer on a journey that ended in Kingussie, where a Venison Distribution Committee had been established, the venison being handed out to poor families in that district.

My reverie about Highland life in the past was shattered by renewed activity in the young forest beyond the Feshie. The saw whined again. Back at the car, I shattered the peace of the glen by over-revving the car engine, which I hoped would startle the hens. When I moved off there must be no wild clucking and no bumps from the wheels!

16

FOOL OF THE MOSS

Achlean is also the starting point for a hard slog beside a burn
known as the Allt Fhearnagan. It leads to the flat, featureless,
altogether sombre crown of Carn Ban Mor (2,445 feet). This and
Sgoran Dubh Mor (3,636 feet) form a major part of a block of
land that dominates Feshie with all the drama of an exclamation
mark. Ban means 'white or fair' and Sgor indicates a 'sharp
rock'.

The other side of the range is even more sharply defined.
Below the beetling crags of Sgoran lies Loch Einich, its surplus
water rippling through a bold glen to the river Spey. Temporary
settlements—shielings—clustered around the head of Loch
Einich in the days when Highland families drove their cattle to
the hills to benefit from a summer flush of grass. Once the loch
was dammed to hold felled timber, which was released down the
burn in favourable times at the start of a journey to the river
mouth.

Friends told me that if I climbed Carn Ban Mor I would see
extensive mossland, not a jumble of naked rock as on Cairn
Gorm. There was the possibility that I would see nothing except
the sodden ground a foot or two away, for clouds often rest on
the hill. What drove me up a very monotonous path to the
summit was the prospect of meeting one of the rarest nesting
birds in Britain. Here, the previous spring, a friend found the
nest of the dotterel (*Eudromias morinellus*).

Every bird-water would like to see a dotterel in its nesting haunt, which means that nowadays there is widespread intrusion of dotterel country—or, at least, its handiest stretches. All I could recall of the dainty and colourful little plover was the sight of a bird in passage. The dotterel had alighted at Spurn Point, on the Yorkshire coast, and did not seem to resent a half circle of bright-eyed ornithologists who surveyed it from not very far away. Now the dotterel, like those other fine Highland birds—golden eagle and capercaillie—has returned to the Lake District. A nest was found by a man who undertook a slog as long and hard as those that are necessary to reach dotterel country in the Central Highlands.

Until I climbed Carn Ban Mor I thought of the dotterel as a bird nesting on austere and rocky plateaux, but it is also found on hills that are well fleshed with peat. The Gaelic name, *t-amadan mointich,* or *mointeach,* means 'the fool of the peat moss'. The *morinellus* of its Latin name means 'simpleton'.

I began to feel a fool when I had been trudging up the hill for over an hour, in mist that did not give me the compensation of seeing fine Highland scenery during the increasingly frequent stops for rest. The journey lasted for over two hours. I became bored by the monotony of the slope, the only light relief being the discovery of an antler cast by a young red deer stag. I could appreciate the dedication of naturalists who walk this way in the winter desolation, though their journey might be enlivened only by the calls of the ever-cheerful snow buntings. I saw a few meadow pipits and a pert cock wheatear. Distant golden plover piped a winsome aria to the spring. The dotterel looks like a small, dark-backed version of the golden plover in summer. And both species, losing the bright nuptial tones after the nesting season, become pale imitations of their former selves.

My reward came instantly at about 3,440 feet. Reaching the rim of Carn Ban Mor, I had only time to make a cursory glance at the grassy summit when I saw a dotterel moving briskly on yellowish legs that seemed to twinkle. The bird stood still for a few seconds. It raised and lowered its slender wings as though it was dissipating some surplus nervous energy.

I felt shocked rather than elated. Good things like dotterels should be hard to find! It would have been better if I had recovered from my exertions; if my excitement had been allowed to rise to fever pitch; if the bird had shown itself towards the end of the expedition. There are many 'ifs' in dotterel-hunting!

My friend, climbing in the previous year, had been even more successful, and with very little extra effort. He had started to walk across the plateau when a dotterel fluttered off its nest, revealing three eggs. The wings and tail were outspread as it moved off along the ground, engrossed in a distraction display. The fortunate bird-watcher looked at the nest and walked on further. He returned to find that the dotterel was again swaddling its eggs. The wife of this exultant bird-watcher recalls that he was emotionally spent. Ignoring her interest in alpine plant life he said, rather gruffly: "Right! Now we can go back down!" And without a further word he strode off Carn Ban Mor!

My dotterel departed with a flicker of wings. When it had gone out of sight, the world seemed empty, desolate, enlivened only by the distant belching of ptarmigan.

I had seen a bird that recently alighted on the roof of Scotland after a journey from wintering grounds by the Mediterranean, where it impresses knowledgeable ornithologists by its sheer numbers. The dotterel colours up with the spring, the crown of its head becoming dark brown, with a white eye stripe boldly displayed and with chestnut and black on the under-parts.

Authorities differ in their assessment of the distribution of the dotterel in Britain in times past. Was there ever a time when it nested regularly, in numbers, south of the Scottish border? The Reverend F. O. Morris, in his *History of British Birds* (1857) gave Westmorland, Cumberland, Northumberland, together with East Lothian, Dumfries, and other parts of Scotland, as nesting places apart from the classic Highland country.

Once, dotterel were senselessly slain during their northward journey. In my native Yorkshire, 'sportsmen' gathered near Reighton, a coastal area, to shoot the birds, which seemed to be fond of lingering in this district. The enterprising publican called his premises the *Dotterel Inn*. When dotterel nested on the Pennines, the increasing rarity of the species attracted egg-collectors. A dalesman wrote to a collector in 1831: "Your application for eggs of the dotterel is at least a month too late. But have you not made a mistake? I think it possible that in the hurry of writing you said 'eggs' instead of 'skins' ". Trips of migrating dotterels were to be seen in the Lake Counties, moving along the coast or over the central fells. A few pairs nested, usually at about 2,500 feet above sea level.

The dotterel is confiding, both on migration and also on the nesting grounds. Yet it is not foolishness that impels a bird to sit so hard on its nest that a man can walk up to it, stroke its back or even lift it from the eggs. Seeing a brooding dotterel is difficult. The ability to remain absolutely still on its nest is a defensive stratagem of considerable importance in austere countryside. To fly is often to court disaster at the talons of a hunting eagle or some other predator. My friend found his dotterel nest because he almost trod on it.

So the dotterel sits tightly. Countless generations of birds have developed an instinctive inclination towards immobility. The brooding bird cannot rely on the warning cries of a mate on sentry duty, which is the case with most other waders. The dainty little dotterel hunched over the eggs is, surprisingly, the cock and not the hen. When the female has laid its clutch of eggs she leaves the task of hatching them out and tending the young to the male! It has been suggested that the male dotterel deserves to be called 'fool of the moss' because it gives the female so much latitude!

The eggs are cryptic—dull, olive-grey eggs with heavy blotching upon them. When most ground-nesting birds slip away from their nests they leave eggs which are difficult to see against the tones of the countryside round about. The cock dotterel sits hard, leaving the eggs for limited periods, when it must feed. Not only must the eggs be kept warm as a matter of necessity, but they must be shielded from the often cruel weather of the high hills, where June frosts are not uncommon. A Speyside naturalist found a nest by accident in June and noticed that the eggs had been badly cracked by frost. The brooding bird must have been killed, its body taken away.

For about 22 days the cock dotterel protects the eggs. Flush the bird from the nest, and it does not go far. Indeed, it lurches forward with partly-open wings, dragging the white-bordered tail along the ground, seeking to distract an intruder from the eggs by claiming all the attention. Dotterel chicks are also masters of the art of total immobility, but when their nerve is broken by someone lingering close by, or touching them, they run nimbly at speed, even through depressions and over tussocks which a man might lightly press underfoot but which, to a bird a few inches tall, are significant obstructions.

I walked around Carn Ban Mor, mindful that almost 200 years ago Colonel Thornton had come this way. He and his friends planned their journey through Glen Feshie to the hills in early August. "At half past four we were awakened, and a finer morning never ushered in the day." The expedition began at 8 am and, finding the Spey was unfordable, its members had to ride over four miles to use the ferry at Ruthven. They entered "the vale of Fische", which was Colonel Thornton's rendering of Glen Feshie.

At 10 am they were "at the foot of the mountain, the heat intense, the mercury standing at 84 Fahrenheit. A severe labour we had to ascend this mountain, as steep as the side of a house; rocky, and sometimes boggy; whilst frequently large stones, on which our horses stept with apparent security, would give way, and whirr down the precipice, so that they were frightened beyond imagination."

At noon, they had reached patches of snow. "Before one we thought we were near the mouth of Glen Ennoch, and then depositing our Champaign, lime, shrub, porter, &c, in one of the large snow-drifts, beneath an arch, from which ran a charming spring, we agreed to dine there."

During the climb, the Colonel's pointers had found some game. He slew "an old moor cock and a ptarmigant, which I ordered to be well-pickled and prepared for dinner". Arriving at the edge of the crags of Sgoran, Colonel Thornton recorded his impressions. "It is impossible to describe the astonishment of the whole party when they perceived themselves on the brink of that frightful precipice which separated them from the lake below!" They remained motionless, "equally struck with admiration and horror".

While his friends descended to the edge of the loch, the Colonel—who had decided the walk would be tedious and severe —attempted to kill a "ptarmigant" or two, simply to pass the time. The exhausted friends returned, and a fresh and lively Colonel Thornton sought to distract them from their aches and pains. Captain Waller was revived when the Colonel, knowing of his interest in ptarmigan, placed one of the birds he had shot in such a position that it appeared to be alive. He pointed it out to the Captain, who shot at it with glee!

For dinner, the main dish consisted of two brace and a half of "ptarmigant", a moorcock, slices of Yorkshire-smoked ham and reindeer's tongue, "with some sweet herbs, &c, prepared by the housekeeper at Raits".

Afterwards, the Colonel recalled the "solemn silence" of Sgoran Dubh Mor, which "soothes the mind with the most agreeable emotion".

17

MONARCHS OF THE GLENS

The late spring evening had darkened into total blackness by
11 pm. Now that even the afterglow of the sun had gone, all
that remained was a calm in which the frost stung. By morning
there would be another crust of ice on the puddles.

With a local man, I drove the car along a private road leading
past a big house and on, with a steadily degenerating surface,
into a deep glen. We motored slowly, car springs twanging, on
a route hemmed in by trees. Beside one of them stood a young
red stag.

The deer's coat appeared lustrous in the headlamp beam,
though a few tatters of the winter suit was still upon it. A
thrustful early growth of new antler was swathed in velvet. The
deer raised its head as though to taste the air, or maybe to look
around rather than through the sudden, disorientating blaze of
light. The air around its muzzle was clouded with vapour which
the animal exhaled. Then the stag had gone—lost to view in
a few yards because of an impenetrable growth of tree and
shrub.

It was not the most romantic way to see a Highland red deer.
I could recall more stimulating occasions. There was the day a
summering group of stags went clattering across one of the high
corries of the Cairngorms; an afternoon with a frosty edge to
it when I flushed some foragers from one of the old 'black woods',
and winter views from the railway about Drumochter Pass of
deer moving in snow not very far from the tracks. The Drum-

L

ochter deer should be provided with extra food by the Tourist
Board, for they have entertained thousands of visitors. Drumochter is primarily a grouse reserve, but red deer enter it from forests
round about.

Everyone who goes to the Highlands on holiday would like to
see the largest, noblest of British mammals moving freely, not
emparked. Most visitors arrive in summer, and they move about
mainly on sunny afternoons. Then all self-respecting deer are
at rest. Red deer, on high ground, lie down and remain still when
they have been alerted. The rust-red of their summer coats
harmonizes with the coarse vegetation round about.

On my springtime jaunt I saw few red deer. There were just
a few parties of hinds, moderately high up. The deer tend to
invade the low ground in winter, and here they find both
shelter and food. A friend who took a ciné camera to the Highlands at snowtime actually braked his car as a large party of red
deer crossed the road ahead. He was able to record the sight on
colour film; the sequence may be poor technically but it does
record some memorable moments.

My most evocative glimpses of red deer have been in early
spring and concern small parties of red deer standing on orange
and brown moorland with the snow-streaked Cairngorms
providing a backdrop. At this time of the year, the Highlands
wear a Joseph's coat of many colours and are visually more
exciting than in summer, when the view seems to be composed
simply of 100 shades of green.

To state baldly that red deer summer on the hill and winter
on low ground creates a distorted picture. The deer ascend the
heights and fall back into the glens in accordance with the
subtle variations of weather and season. A stag on a hillside is
a natural barometer.

Theoretically, it should be possible to find red deer at any time
in the Highlands. Scotland has a population of about 180,000
deer in the estimation of the Red Deer Commission, and by far
the greatest number live north of the Highland line. How does
one estimate the numbers of a species which is so devious and
is spread over millions of acres of rough country?

Lord Arbuthnott, speaking as chairman of the Red Deer Commission, explained that the figure is arrived at by first assessing the distribution of red deer and the total area of ground occupied by them, about seven million acres. Thereafter, the acreage covered by the annual counts (4,190,000 acres by the end of 1969) gives as accurate a figure as possible for deer known to lie within the counted areas.

Finally, an estimate is made of the deer density within the major uncounted areas, of which there are presently five, and a total is achieved. The areas counted include some that have been re-counted once or more, and allowance is made in the total for any change discernible. Each year also the estimate of deer numbers on uncounted areas is checked in the knowledge of actual first counts over any new area. It's simple!

There are now too many red deer for the land available, given the present state of management. The fault lies with man, not the deer. A population explosion occurred among Highland deer when stalking became popular, and the number of deer forests grew; when not only were the beasts protected and encouraged to breed without restraint, but the sportsman took only the best stags. Few hinds were culled. One ecologist has stated that in his view a reasonable stocking of red deer today might be 80,000.

To go out on the hill with a Highland stalker is a stimulating if exacting experience. Lying almost flat on his back, with his telescope resting on a crook, he is watchful, taciturn, intent, for maybe a quarter of an hour while his guest scans treeless country and marvels that any creature can lie there unobserved. Suddenly, the stalker's vigil is over. He gives the location of the deer and also points out the most suitable stags for culling. It is no wonder that the average summer visitor hears with disbelief of the number of deer in the areas he has toured. He has not got the stalker's eye.

Even more remarkable is the ability of the good stalker to take a novice so close to grazing deer that he can actually hear the sound made as they tear at the herbage. The stalker is never in a hurry. He measures the duration of an expedition in hours rather than minutes. He never breaks the skyline, and knows the habits of the deer almost as well as the deer themselves. For instance, Highland reds tend to stand with high ground rising behind them. They invariably face into the wind. Other beasts and the birds of the hills provide, by their calling and sudden flight, an early-warning system that the deer exploit to the full. They also have some finely-tuned senses—of hearing, smell, sight.

The layman does not pay enough regard to the direction of the wind. Naturally, he will move into the wind, but it can play tricks in the hill country, with currents broken up by the peaks, converging again from several directions. On slack days, there are merely eddies of wind. The merest whiff of human scent, curling over a ridge or spreading out on a broad front, can alert deer over half a mile away. In the former case, a party of deer might depart without having been seen by the intruder.

Scent is all-important. "Above all things, let not the devil tempt you to trifle with a deer's nose," wrote the brothers Stuart in *Lays of the Deer Forest* (1848). "You may cross his sight, walk up to him in a grey coat or, if standing against a tree or rock near your own colour, wait till he walks up to you, but you cannot cross his nose even at an incredible distance, but he will feel the tainted air."

They doubly emphasized the point. "Colours and forms may be deceptive or alike . . . but there is but one scent of Man and that he never doubts or mistakes; that is filled with danger and terror; and one whiff of its poison at a mile off—his nose to the wind—and the next moment his antlers turn and he is away to the hill or wood—and he may not be seen on the same side of the forest for a month."

Red deer endure in numbers because they have been readily adaptable to changing conditions of food and terrain. British red deer vary in size and weight. At one extreme are the well-fed, coddled park deer, and at the other the smaller Highland reds, beasts that are so distinctive following centuries of hard life in poor terrain that some early naturalists were inclined to allot to them a special subspecies—*Cervus elaphus scoticus*.

Their main sanctuary has been the 'deer forest', which is a

forest in the medieval sense—a chase for wild beasts. A Scottish deer forest might be country without a single tree. Fortunately for the deer, there were tracts of land too remote from the main haunts of man to make sheep-grazing an economical proposition and, in some cases, altogether too bare to be developed as preserves for sporting birds like grouse. They became dedicated to deer. Colonel Thornton wrote: "In general, [deer forests] mean large hills, having good grass; they are kept undisturbed, and of course the red deer, being quick, prefer these boundaries, but not a tree is to be seen".

When puny men first hunted and fished in Britain, the red deer were already well established as members of the native fauna. They have been here for perhaps 400,000 years. There were giants in those days! The early reds might be compared to wapiti, now the largest of the Cervus genus, which stand 5 feet or more at the withers and can weigh up to 1,000 pounds. The modern reds are small by comparison with these and also with some Continental races, from which they became separated when the land bridge between Britain and the Continent sank. About 1840 the Monadhliath deer were reputed to be the largest in Scotland, a state accounted for by the abundance of herbs and species of fungus.

For thousands of years before the coming of man (and, indeed, for many years afterwards, man being at first a frail and fumbling creature), red deer shared a rich habitat with mammals that have long been extinct. Highland reds were the neighbours of brown bear, wolf, giant elk and beaver. The wolves were most significant, for when they packed in late winter they pursued and dragged down the weakest of the deer.

Once, the red deer were found as free-ranging beasts over most of Britain, being numerous in lowland Scotland, where—in due course—man cleared the tree cover and established his many settlements. The red deer survived in the hillier north and became primarily creatures of the open hillside. Dr Peter Delap, who has studied the red deer for many years, asserts that they were not primarily forest beasts and used the marginal land. The spread up into Scotland took place a little ahead of the main colonization by trees. Red deer, indeed, followed the edge of the tree line, which was generally much higher than it is today.

When man slew the last wolves in the early part of the eighteenth century, he remained the only significant predator on deer. Royalty and clan chiefs had hunted the deer with hounds, summoning large numbers of retainers to drive the beasts into selected areas. Deer were poached by ordinary folk. They were a good source of fresh meat during a lean winter. By the end of the eighteenth century, the deer population was low and many of their ancestral feeding grounds had been invaded by the ubiquitous sheep. Only a dozen 'deer forests' existed in the whole of Scotland in 1790.

The situation was reversed when sheep became less attractive propositions than they had been when first introduced in numbers. And deer-stalking became popular. Several factors speeded stalking into prominence. Books were written by those who found pleasure in the sport. The quality and reliability of firearms improved. And the new-rich of England's industrial revolution became attracted to the notion of sojourning in the wild but beautiful Highlands, seeking deer through healthy exercise, breathing crisp mountain air. This trend became formalized when Queen Victoria and dear Albert became more Scottish than the Scots, and Balmoralism arose.

Now there was a diminishing demand for deerhounds and for large groups of men. The ghillie came into his own. A quickening demand for stalking facilities was a godsend to the Highland lairds, many of whom had fallen on hard times. Now their estates were valuable properties. It was important to preserve deer, and this trend is reflected in the history of the Duke of Atholl's estate. Less than 100 red deer inhabited the Forest of Atholl in 1776, but the number had risen to over 5,000 in about 1845. Those who advertised Gaick Forest for sale in 1812 had the new ideas in mind, announcing that Gaick "is adopted for summer grazing of black cattle, or for shooting ground to a sportsman who might wish to preserve a tract for deer".

The prophet of the new age was William Scrope, who spent a decade hunting deer in a Perthshire forest and then wrote *The*

Art of Deerstalking (1845). Scrope described "a very interesting pursuit as nearly as possible in the style and spirit in which I have always seen it carried on. . . . The beautiful motions of the deer, his picturesque and noble appearance, his sagacity and the skilful generalship which can alone ensure success in the pursuit of him, keep the mind in a constant state of pleasurable excitement."

Sporting interests benefited from the improvement in Highland roads, in addition to which new estate roads were laid down, bridges built, and lodges constructed so that the wealthy visitors would have home comforts at the end of the day. By 1912, when the modern saga of the Highland reds was reaching its peak of popularity among sportsmen, there were 203 deer forests in Scotland, representing 3½ million acres. Just before the outbreak of the 1914–18 war, deer-stalking had become the most lucrative sport in the Highlands. Almost three million acres of deer forest existed in 1955.

The sport had its opponents—not those who objected to field sports as such, but groups like the crofters who, being especially vocal in the north and west of Scotland, objected to playing second fiddle to a wild animal. One of the first Crofters' Commissions, in 1884, recommended that deer forests should be limited, but no parliamentary action was taken.

The 1914–18 war, which destroyed much of the old social order, worked against the interests of the deer. Lairds had difficulty in letting many forests, and deer were killed to provide food for a beleagured island people. Into the forests came cattle and sheep that would also contribute to the national larder. Stalking rallied again after the war but then its popularity declined, so that by the beginning of the 1939–45 war sheep were popular again. During the war the conditions that obtained in the first international conflict applied again. Deer were hunted for the meat they could provide and not primarily for sport.

A notable piece of legislation in 1959 was the passing of the Deer (Scotland) Act. Under it a Red Deer Commission was established to advise the Secretary of State for Scotland on all matters relating to red deer. It has some important powers and can, for instance, keep a check on the number of deer slain, also take action against marauding deer which damage crops. Close seasons were introduced.

From the middle of the eighteenth century, thoughtful land-owners set about afforestation with a zest that has not been fully appreciated. Then, from the end of the 1914–18 war, the Forestry Commission moved in, becoming the major landowner and converting 826,000 acres of Scotland into coniferous forest. The deer could be a nuisance, damaging young trees, and so the new plantations were fenced against them, the current cost of fencing being between £600 and £700 a mile.

Self-preservation impels the Highland red to seek out new forestland when they are particularly hungry. There is a period, in February and March, when all the deer face starvation. The landscape is barren, its vegetation wizened, lacking in sufficient protein to maintain the beasts effectively. The time of the spring-time growth of fresh shoots is not yet at hand. Mortality is usually high in spring.

Red deer, following the old trods into the glens, come up against much deer fencing. This happens to the south of Avie-more where deer frustrated by fencing are seen milling around on the snowy Great North Road at night. Collisions between deer and vehicles are not uncommon.

The fittest deer survive the winter depredation and also the brisk culling undertaken by man. Springtime brings a flush of new grass to the hills. The deer begin to put on weight again. When I was in the Highlands, the survivors had regained their fitness. The hinds would stay together as groups, wandering but little from the areas they favoured. The stags have their separate but less-well-defined territories; they are more nomadic than the hinds.

Generally, the moult starts in May, but nature does not always accede to man-made calendar dates. There would be, among the corries of the Cairngorms, some stags with the tattered look of beasts still shedding the winter coat in unsightly tufts. Some, indeed, would still be moulting winter hair in mid-summer.

Stags cast their horns from mid-March to early May, and immediately the growth of new horn begins, with the sensitive tissues swaddled in the tough but pliant hairy skin called velvet. Stags growing new antlers try to avoid flies partly because of the irritation caused by the biting varieties to the new, still soft antlers.

Mature stags and hinds intermingle for only about six weeks, the time of the rut, and apart from this period the deer lead placid lives as remote as possible from man. A group of females will include an old hind wise to the ways of the hills. This animal readily barks a warning to the others when alarmed. Calves are dropped in early June, a time of mainly settled weather. Weighing 14 or 15 pounds at birth, couched in heather, the new calf struggles to its gangling legs at the start of a hill life that will never be easy.

In the third week in September, the main drama of the Highland reds begins. The stags, now in 'clean horn', have arrived at the hind ground. Each stag musters as many hinds as it can, and with this harem it moves around the hills. A stag roars a challenge to other stags.

October is the main month of the 'roaring'. A forester I met in Glen Feshie urged me to return in October. "Get up on the hills on a misty day. Find one of the corries. Settle down to watch and listen." A corrie—as I recall—can be like an echo-chamber. "When a red deer roars," said the forester, "you'll shiver with the excitement of it."

Picture a rutting stag, caked from wallowing in places where the peat has been stirred up until it is like dark porridge. The animal is bleary-eyed from lack of sleep. It has not been feeding regularly. Its mighty antlers may be festooned with vegetation it has ripped from the ground during short periods of wild thrashing. Now it lifts up its head so that its antlers almost stroke its back—and finds its voice, a roaring that is capable of stirring up many echoes.

After the rut, there is another winter to face. And death strikes often these days. About 25,000 Highland reds are culled every year, for to keep the population under control in existing circumstances it is necessary to destroy a sixth of the population of each sex, excluding the calves.

Old history is repeating itself in the Highlands. In the early days, man hunted for venison, a valuable source of protein in winter when all the domestic stock apart from a breeding nucleus was killed and salted down. There were years when the Highland deer existed to produce wealthy men with sporting trophies, and often it was too much trouble to cart a carcass from the hill. It was left for the eagles, crows and ravens.

Today, flesh is the main requirement. The Red Deer Commission observed in 1969 that "the overall increase in the value of red deer both as a sporting trophy and as a meat-producing animal ensures that they are able to make a valuable contribution to the economic prosperity of upland Scotland". The same report noted a significant fall in the number of Highland reds.

British venison is plentiful, but less than 5 per cent of it is consumed at home. Over 1,800 tons are exported to Germany every year. Germans tuck into meals of Highland venison while Britons dine on beef and mutton, the latter with mint sauce. Highland venison costs between 10p and 19p a pound, which means that a single carcass is worth a considerable sum, say about £20. Selective culling of deer is one thing, and the ruthless shooting of deer as a cash crop, much of it by poachers, is another and less desirable element in the story.

Venison is an acquired taste. It is a dark meat with very little fat. Precautions must be taken during cooking or the meat will dry out. The Scottish 'October stag' gives venison a bad name, for the older the beast the stronger is the flavour, and wild beasts have more flavour than park beasts. A friend challenged my assertion that venison is tough by writing: "Take note—I've just had a chunk of red calf for my tea—delicious!"

Landseer gave us all a fellow-feeling for deer when he painted *Monarch of the Glen*. The original of that painting is now owned by a whisky firm, which has reproduced it extensively in its advertising. We see on the famous picture a podgy, contented beast with a wonderful backdrop, the High Cairngorms.

Today we must reconcile the conflicting interests of trees,

deer, sheep and sentiment. Whatever happens, the red deer will be neither as numerous nor as widespread as it was in the heyday of the Highland deer forests, when preservation and limited sporting activity were the rules. It would, of course, be unthinkable for Scotland to lose its stately monarchs of the glens.

INDEX